Collected Poems

Francis Harvey

First published in 2007
The Dedalus Press
13 Moyclare Road
Baldoyle
Dublin 13
Ireland

www.dedaluspress.com

ISBN 978 1 904556 67 1 (bound)
ISBN 978 1 904556 68 8 (paper)

Dedalus Press titles are represented in North America
by Syracuse University Press, Inc., 621 Skytop Road,
Suite 110, Syracuse, New York 13244, and in the UK by
Central Books, 99 Wallis Road, London E9 5LN

Printed and bound in the UK by Lightning Source,
6 Precedent Drive, Rooksley, Milton Keynes MK13 8PR, UK

Typesetting / design by Pat Boran
with thanks to Noel Duffy
Cover image, *Beached hulk in Derrybeg Bay, Co. Donegal*
© Janine Bolliger

The Dedalus Press receives financial assistance from
An Chomhairle Ealaíon / The Arts Council, Ireland

Collected Poems

Francis Harvey

To Ger, Deirdre, & Fergus
in memory of Ger Blackstone days
Francis Harvey

Dedalus

ACKNOWLEDGEMENTS

Acknowledgements are due to the editors of the following in which a number of these poems, or versions of them, originally appeared:

Cork Literary Review, Cyphers, The Honest Ulsterman, Irish Pages, The Irish Times, Kilkenny Magazine, New Irish Writing: The Irish Press, Poetry Review Review and *The SHOp*.

In memory of my sister, Anne

Contents

New Poems

Introduction
by Moya Cannon

As the title of his first book, *In the Light on the Stones*, suggests, Francis Harvey's work is grounded in a celebration of landscape and of light, the tumble and abundance of light, most particularly on the mountains of south Donegal, which he has walked, alone or in the company of his wife or children, and which he conjures for us as Norman McCaig conjured the mountains and the mountain lakes of Sutherland, or as R.S. Thomas gave us the austere valleys of Wales:

> It is going down the mountain
> again after going up
> past the high lakes
>
> most never see
> that aches in the heart
> like love lost.
>
> 'Selves'

Vividness and lucidity are his hall-marks, often the vividness of winter light after a long day's hill-walking, when every detail of a mountainside is cast into relief:

> I check my route and
> watch a hare white
> in its winter coat
> sit back in a gap of light
> scanning a stone whose
> lichen maps
> worlds
> unknown to me and
> cartography.
>
> 'Map Lichen on Slievetooey'

1

A haiku-like combination of attention and playfulness throughout, reminiscent of the hare's own darts and shifts of direction, serves to animate the work. Odd juxtapositions alert us, as in 'Hail and Farewell', where he writes of the birth of a bull-calf — "all sea-legs after nine months afloat…" and of the death of his mother's brother on the same day:

> And me listening to him
> grinding out the last sounds he'd ever make
> in this world from the depths of his throat like stones
> scraping the keel as Charon launched his boat.

The power of this work derives, largely, from a perfect marriage of imagery and rhythm, as the mysterious emotive energies of assonance and onomatopoeia are brought into play and rhyme is allowed to hammer the heart open:

> Something utterly true to itself, a stone being a stone,
> is plunging into its shadow and the mouse's flesh and bone
> 'Kestrel'

The rendered beauty of the landscapes which he sees with a painter's eye is all the more convincing because he does not flinch from the harshness of the granite landscapes or from the material poverty of the lives lived by the sheep farmers who cling to them. Some of his best-known and best-loved poems constitute a group of elegies for the solitary old people who lived in the mountain valleys of south Donegal, the people who, like 'The Last Drover', "left no deeds or songs at all". Only someone of Harvey's compassion could reconstruct, out of this very absence, the essence of the humanity of these men and women. This he does without either sentimentality or a pity which could be read as patronization. He affords these survivors of decayed communities the dignity of understated tragedy. He shows how they were, literally, bonded to their land, as in 'The Death of Thady' —

> He could not tell you why,
> he loves the place so much – and
> love's a word he would never use…..

or in 'The Deaf Woman in the Glen' —

> ...she is
> locked in this
> landscape's fierce
>
> embrace as
> the badger is whose
> unappeasable jaws only
>
> death unlocks from
> the throat of rabbit
> or rat and
>
> moves, free yet
> tethered,
> through
> time's inexorable weathers.

This compassion is also manifest in the many poems which refer, directly or indirectly, to the northern troubles. Born in Enniskillen to a Presbyterian father, who died when Harvey was six years old, and to a Catholic mother, he was better placed than most to experience and articulate the pain of both communities.

> Loyal Iniskilling or
> Inis Ceithleann, fierce
> Ceithleann's island,
> forged me true.
>   'Mixed Marriage'

One would be tempted to say that Francis Harvey's work combines the passion for precision of a naturalist and the yearning for grace of a poet, except for the fact that a passion for precision, for naming, is also part of the bedrock of poetry. In the later poems there is a vivid sense of how we are all moving, "free but tethered, through time's inexorable weathers." In the context of Irish poetry, Francis Harvey is a Basho-like figure, guided by an unwavering sense of true north, always moving to the washed light on higher ground.

3

from **In the Light on the Stones**

Death of Thady

He could not tell you why
he loves the place so much—and
love's a word that he would never use.

He could not tell you why
there is no other place where
he walks taller than Errigal
and plants his feet like dolmens
in a wind-scoured land of scant grass and scanter sky.

He could not tell you why,
when he lay ailing in the warm bright ward,
the dark glens and the lonely
lakes in the sky and the flagged
cabin cold and bare as a prison-cell,
were heaven to him as sure as this was hell.

He could not tell you why,
after the priest had gone
and the nurse indifferently watched him die,
he suddenly saw the hill-wind swirling
the turf-mould on the ward-room floor
and counted the last of his sheep filing
like mourners through the gap of the door.

Fossil

They make a space for him who inhabits space
as a star inhabits the loneliness of it.
He stands on his own at the back of the thronged hall,
a long great-coat corded round the cairn of his body.
He steams in the heat and a pool of dampness gathers
about him and the sheepdog lying at his feet.
The peaked cap's a fungus growing out of his head,
the black rubber boots are bollards of eroded peat.
He lights up with hunched shoulders, huge hands cupped
round the bowl of the pipe, the sound of the wind that matts
wisps of the Grey Mare's Tail on the haunches of Suhill
whorled in his ears for ever like the sea in a shell.
Smoke clouds the weathered granite of his face.
Suddenly the dog pricks up its ears, watching
his lips, waiting for a signal from him
to rout this pen of bleating sheep good
for neither dipping nor shearing.
But its master dreams, has a rapt faraway
look in his eyes as if already nostalgic for
the vast acreage of sky outside. He's calculating
the price he should get for his ewes at Brockagh Fair.

The Last Drover

For fifty years he travelled light into
every kind of darkness and saw more
winter dawns than was good for man or beast.

He wore the same serge suit summer
and winter indifferent as a whin bush
to the wind and rain that bent him in the end.

He slept on his feet like them listening
for the silences that woke him when
they softened through a gap or

bunched in sudden terror of a shadow.
He knew the stones of his roads better
than the corns on his feet.

Their heat warmed him on bitter nights.
They lowed to their own kind across stone walls and ditches.
He talked out loud to himself in the dark.

I mourn him now who left no deeds or songs
to set against the curlew's desolating cry at dawn,
who left no deeds or songs at all.

Elegy for the Islanders

They died elsewhere but their graves are here
and these bare gables are their head-stones.

Their strong hearts faltered long before their
roof-beams fell and their hearth-stones, cold

as their bones in an alien earth, mourn the memory
of their fires in diamonds of black.

I walk on the lichened stones of their graves
and a split flag cracks as their hearts cracked

once. I hear their death-rattles deep down
in the gullet of the sound and taste the salt

of their tears on the wind. Tears will wear out
a stone but what will a heart wear out but itself?

They wore out their hearts and left nothing here
but stones washed by the tides of their tears.

Mixed Marriage

Loyal Inniskilling or
Inis Ceithleann, fierce
Ceithleann's island,
forged me true: bred

its acid loam into my
soul: sconced acres
lapped by dividing
waters, turbulent

pools too deep for
stepping-stones or gods
to fathom and sheughs
softer than love that

sprung the traps baited
when two faiths mate
and bridge islands
unknown to Ceithleann.

Fare thee well, Inniskilling!
Fare thee well, Inis Ceithleann!
I come of bridge-builders whose
stones, plumb, spanned more than water.

Manus

Was it for this
he enriched her body with a spendthrift
abandon his lean acres craved in lime
yet broke her on a standing stone
as hard and inexorable as Time?

Was it for this
he took crop his loins had sown
on flesh and bone and shipped it overseas
like bags of Banner seed then limed the land
too late for beasts no son of his would need?

Was it for this
he cast her, spent as a kelt, alongside
the corpse of her stillborn tenth child
and hardened his heart against the knife of a wind
sharper than March hones on the hills of Disert?

Was it for this
he tholed the gnawing teeth of the seasons
that stripped his spirit to the bone until
it was as cold as a granite boulder
the glacier once scoured out of Gaguin?

To stand alone
in his doorway at nightfall and watch, high above
dewfall and hawkfall, the sky seeded with stars
as barren as he wished in Christ's name his own
seed had been all the times he'd opened her for another lost crop.

An Oak in the Glen

He is ploughing
the lea field
with the brown mare
the way
his father and
his father's father
ploughed it;

he is taking
the burn hill
under a streamer of gulls
the way
his father and
his father's father
took it;

he is stooping
under a yoke
heavier than his mare's
the way
that stunted oak
stoops in the wind
from the sea;

the way
it was stooped
in the wind
from the sea
when his father
and his father's father
ploughed this lea;

the way
it will still be stooped
in the wind
from the sea
when his children and
his children's children
plough this lea.

In Memory of Patrick MacGill 1890—1963

Childhood was the rainbow you knew would end
for good at the foot of the glen. Over-
night Strabane made a man of you the hard
way; no more crocks of gold then. You'd sold your
body to the highest bidder but your spirit
would always be inviolate to grosser men;
the best thing you could do now was
to put it all down in words: glensmen
cast like seed on the four winds;
the magic in the light at certain times
of day; those hills full of lakes, sheep, silence;
the rushy holms stippled with sunlight and flowers;
Christ on your lips at Mass; the chrism
of wonder transfiguring every stone and
blade of grass until they became a part
of you ever after in Glasgow, London,
the trenches, New York.

When you died in exile years later were
the fibres and splinters still festering in your heart?

Condy

He lives alone in the shadow of
mountains; his tilted stony acres
fray the clouds; he takes
eight years out of a dog and knows
his ewes better than the sons
he never had. The horizon is
his fence, his sheep range free
and yet his mind is
penned, his spirit tethered. He climbs
through darkness into
the light on summits but hears
no voices from a cloud. He fears
death—the rickle of bleached
bones in lonely places—and in drink
weeps for himself and his brothers
and for all the others
on whom the shadow of mountains
fell.

Brendan in Donegal

He could forget the malice of cities:
Whispered knives in his back on every street:
London, Paris, New York, Dublin: pities
And glories still triggering heart and feet.

For him, each evening, rainbows arched our skies,
The glens were blue-belled, magpies flew in pairs;
Tinkers and sheepmen eyed him with surprise:

15

A ribald cherub sampling country airs.
He came on tidal waves of talk; the moor,
Island, quay, and pub, our native sounds, were drowned
In saltier seas; and when he left we found

The certain marks of a leviathan.
But the first trippers, stumbling on the spoor
Of genius, showed us the footprints of a man.

In The Light On The Stones In The Rain

Mostly, in West Donegal,
it is rock and light, and water, but rock above all,
and rain, to-day it is rain, rain falling softly in veils
on foxglove and fuchsia and furze;
and, plaintively calling all day by the sea,
in the mist and the spray,
back and forth in the rain wheel the birds,
plover and curlew and teal.
And then there are men,
in the light on the stones in the rain,
sometimes men, but not often,
for mostly in West Donegal
it is rock and light, and water, not men,
and to-day, to-day it is rain, rain falling softly in veils
on foxglove and fuchsia and furze,
and on birds.

Gates

We're a people who do not love gates, we
are lovers of gaps,
all sorts of oddly-shaped gaps,
gaps in the crochet of lime-stone walls,
gaps in the clouds and the hills,
we are lovers of space,
and our only concession to gates is
a bush or a broken old bed
that creaks in the wind from the Croaghs.
And that's as it should be—
except for the fact that, me,
at times I get tired and I like what I see
so much—a gap with a twenty-mile view to the sea—
I feel I could do with a rest for a while,
just something to lean on and stare—
and a gate, for example, would do.
That's all we think they are good for.

Map Lichen On Slievetooey

Up on this bare summit
where fierce weathers pare
heather and peat down
to its skeletal bone
until the cairns groan
like gods in labour
I check my route and
watch a hare white

in its winter coat sit
back in a gap of light
scanning a stone whose
lichen maps
worlds
unknown to me and
cartography.

Snow

We woke this winter's day to snow
brimming the room with light
and silence and rose to a world
of white perfection: a tree furred with
ermine, a row of icicles barbing the eave-run
of the barn, the sun on a fleece of immaculate
lawn tracked with a bird's italics.

Information For Tourists

Pull up your car for a moment, stranger,
look hard at that broken discarded man
who totters on sticks between the mountain
and the sea. Once he was strong and upright
as you or me till, scraping in the scraw
of his few acres here at home or tatie-
hoking in an icy Scottish mist

from dawn to dusk took all the sweetness
out of him and left this husk. He shares his crust
with no one now, his wife a rickle of misshapen
bones under thin salt clay and stone, his seed,
seed of his loins that didn't fall on barren
Rosses rock and soil, long borne on bitter tides
of grief into the ghettos of half-a-dozen
capital cities and never his own.
Remember Thady when your camera whirrs
on seascape and empty glen, for he too played some part,
who let them make this place a playground for you
out of his desolation of heart.

More Information for Tourists

A beach of stones disgorged
from the maw of the sea.
No doubt you will pause,
stranger, to take due note
of how marvellously
round the sea's shaped and ground
each separate stone smooth as bone.
You will remark the sea's guttural
undertones, the stones
in its throat as well as the stones
it has coughed up on the shore
and the wrecked boat, of course,
and shattered lobster pots
and blobs of spittle and phlegm
the sea's spat out of its mouth
and the sheep-cropped grass track

it has spewed with wrack.
But you, stranger, no matter how
long *you* look you'll never see what I saw
that day the sea sickened in storm and,
clearing its gut, later threw up
the dismembered corpse of Sean Ownie
Ban beside his own wrecked boat,
his face white as the bleached bone of
his severed right hand, a wreath
of sea-weed matted through his hair.
I was there, stranger, and I took due note:
a place I'll remember, God knows,
our beach of stones, that corpse and boat,
till the last ebb-tide rattles
like stones in my own throat.

Dallas: The Nightmare Frontier

He rode into the scrub lands of that last
Frontier unarmed against such lawless law.
On every trail unsaddled stallions passed
Him, wild-eyed, screaming; at noon he saw

The lynched sheriff's enormous shadow swing
Across the sun; wagons of liquor, guns,
Inflamed the tribes, while the last posse hung
Back and watched the ritual slaughter of its sons.

Brazen on every street the killers stood
Jingling their spurs like bangled whores; the court-
House blazed, the judge was shot, and one report

Spoke of another scalping in the South—
Until a new assassin mapped in blood
Darker frontiers where Babel shuts Truth's mouth.

Dorothy Wordsworth in Belfast

To see things as they are:
the blood in a harvest star:
how the tilted light falls
along the corrie walls
and a wind Heaven-tall
dimples the lake like a gong
and bends the long grasses
in the mountain passes;
to possess the seeing eye,
clear as a rain-washed sky,
enraptured by trivia
like *Pyrola Media*,
the hieroglyphics of birds,
Coleridge's magical words,
the texture of the sand
on a smoking wind-swept strand:
Dorothy Wordsworth had such an eye,
not William, not you and I,
but how would it operate
on such minutiae of hate
as the cigarette-burns on the head
of this youth they've just found dead?

The Lament of a Northern Ireland Child

Did they once cry for their mothers
like you or me in terror after

dark, play games, sing and
dance, or was their laughter

maniacal, did they howl like
wolves at the full moon;

do I sometimes meet them like
ordinary people on our street at noon,

do they change shape at night,
sprout horns and grow hooves?

I think they inhabit some special kind
of Hell, neither here nor in the South,

and fear I may one day have to shake the hand that blew
a crater in Johnnie's head the size of his mouth.

Bogside '69

History walled them out. For three centuries,
shabby, down-at-heel, they hung about
the gates of that unbreached
maiden city—such turbulent suitors—cold, preached
at, reviled, their hearts a prey to passion's
ambivalence, their upturned pikes
instruments of love and hate. But she remained

impregnably virgin, her maiden-
head impervious to such crude
assaults—until suddenly last summer their mood
changed and they took her so
violently that every stone they hurled
was the stone of their hearts
echoing and re-echoing round the world.

Swift

Was it that *education of a dog*
Unfitted him to ape those suaver wits
Settling for slippered sex and gout? Some rich bog-
Trotting bishop's only child prone to fits

Of gloom? Formalities of love and hate
He mocked passionately, fearing passion's
Incandescence in the child-menaced state
Of marriage, haunted by dark compassions.

A greater master ruled whose irony
Was final: Time's sane children spoke, acclaimed
The claw-marked prose as magical, then tamed,

Embraced this tiger like a nursery toy,
And when it snarled some raw obscenity
Appalled their parents with their shrieks of joy.

Patrick Kavanagh

Steam from the Mucker dung-heap mists his mind
In Baggot street, condensing into dreams
Of innocence in haunted fields. The wind
That shakes the bed-head in the gap streams

From the stars and God will seed the spirit
With it yet. The pits in winter rise like mounds
To buried kings; the mire and clobber set
Hard with frost; and over the hill the sound

Of Markey's cart jolting in frozen ruts pulls
At the heart. And girls are roses in the light
Of lime-washed walls and still the fiend each night

Breaks loose into the crotch of death and drools till day
Re-yokes the ploughman to the broken earth and gulls,
Like angels round his head, acclaim the clay.

A Picked Bone

The wet limestone
pitted
by sea and rain
and the tears of exiles
glitters
like broken glass in a sudden
avalanche of light that melts
the mist from the glistening

crevice-flowers and strips
the great-breasted
hills up to the very tips
of their nipples where
the hawk has it all
to himself now as he sits
on the wind and broods
on his shadow and
the mouse he will shortly
kill as it waits by the weed-
choked hearth of the roofless
house for the crumbs that will
never come;
the hawk has it all
to himself now as craw-full
at dusk he drifts down-wind
over an island plucked
clean of people
as a stone or
a picked bone.

The Kestrel

is quartering the hill all day with murderous intent.
There is something up there whose heart will never relent.

Look how it rides the vicious swell that rocks it in mid-air.
A fierce rapt contemplation is brooding on something up there.

The mouse shivers in the shadow shivering on the grass:
The only cloud in the rain-scoured sky that will never pass.

Something utterly true to itself, a stone being a stone,
Is plunging into its shadow and the mouse's flesh and bone.

Is it the inexorably professional way it is done
Earns accolades from the larks melting into the sun?

The Caul

for Pauline

You came up in the doctor's trawl that day:
you and your twin sister in the same net:
fish out of water, drowning in air, two
spring-run six-pound salmon, slippery, wet.

But *you* were born with a caul on your head,
a lucky charm against drowning at sea.
Before you touched the deck the doctor had
your birth-cap promised to Nahor the Quay.

Sometimes when we're sailing to the islands
and the half-decker lurches in a squall
I look at you and wish we'd kept that cap:
once is enough to come up in a trawl.

At Ards

All day the pheasants were honking
like vintage cars and
the cows cropped
young grass with a sound
of rending cloth. The ferns
were uncurling their croziers under
the candelabra of the chestnuts and
the hills were blue, blue
as the pools of bluebells in the grass. There was
a smell of crushed
almonds in the airs eddying
from the whins
and you were there
with a flower in your hand and I
was with you and I wanted
to take your other hand but
the children were there
as well and the cows.
I knew they would stare.

Company

I remember the time—
did we really *walk* on air? —
when all that I longed for
was that you be there.

O that was long ago when
the wind was in our hair and
we walked the mountain roads
and no one else was there.

But now we are older and
no longer walk on air
when we walk the mountain roads
someone else is there.

At Ards Again

for Joan

Walking all day in the woods with you,
mile after mile with nothing to say,
except to show you the April beeches

budded with talons like birds of prey;
walking all day through the pines and birches,
mile after mile in the sun and the rain,

what can I say at the end of the journey
but when will we walk in the woods again,
mile after mile with nothing to say?

A Sapling Birch

You have grown out of our reach:
a seed sown long ago now
tall as this sapling birch. I
measure the infinite distance:
fingers of wind in the leaves like
my hands in your hair; a misty
April dawn resonant with bird-
song; our bedroom and the stranger
we welcomed there. So much you
owe to love's climate of kiss
and touch, the soil that nourished you,
the embracing light: remember this.
I hand you over to your lover now
to grow a seedling out of that good earth.
Grow it, grow it and let us rejoice
that you have grown out of our reach.
Out of the good earth grow a sapling birch.

Elegy For A Robin

Something that doesn't belong up here any
more lies on its back in the grass down there.
This tiny foreign body is clogging
the bitter currents of boisterous winter air.

A berry of blood has congealed on its beak
like a haw on this hedge now out of its reach
and I think of all those birds long dead whose songs
sweetened my songs before I soured into speech.

O cold this breeze that plumped its feathers once
and now stirs a claw thin as a filament.
I shiver but *live* in these alien fields.
Only the dead are out of their element.

from **The Rainmakers**

The Rainmakers
for Esther

We shake the young birches
hung with fat raindrops:
local showers that drench
only you and me; witch
doctors, I know, do it
better but this is
personal rainmaking,
private weather. Listen
to the laughter of myself
and my daughter under
the dripping birches.

Lough Eske Wood: The Blue Mist

Nothing much ever happens up here
in the stones and grass: a nondescript brambly
place full of saplings of hazel and ash,
you could pass it for most of the year with
barely a glance. Of course, if you really
fancied the place enough, you could sit there all day
in the sun and the rain and a ram-lamb
or ewe-lamb might dance you a jig
on the grass to the tune of a bird, or
a pheasant might crow, or the wind from the sea grow
lonely listening to the sound of its own
lonely voice. Nothing much ever happens

up here, as I say, until one day
of sun and shadows maybe, looking up through the trees,
you stand transfixed to see in the distance
a blue mist shimmering and floating in the breeze
as veil after veil of bluebells tremulously dare
to match the new shade of Spring a shower's
just washed into the May skies.

Print

I pause to rest on James's drystone wall
that's so low his meadow grass and flowers
crowd all over it when they're summer tall
and envy only the foxglove towers.

But something's happened since I sat here last—
I smelt the sweetness half a field away—
and what was yesterday grass and flowers
now, under the August sun, turns to hay.

And I know by the shape the windrows take
as sure as you'd know the print of a thumb
that James, for the first time ever, hasn't
taken a scythe to his meadow in Lacrum.

The Deaf Woman In The Glen

for Robert Bernen

In her own silence
in the silence
of the glen she is

a stone accepting
rain, a thorn bent
under the weight

of the wind, a heap
of bleached bones
in the gullet

of a dry burn. She has
hair whiter than
Scardan has in

winter; feldspar is
the pink grained
in the granite

of her cheeks; clouds
shadow the unplumbed
peat-brown

of her eyes and, perched
on this outcrop
of rock outside her

door and native
to her station as
the raven to its

crag, she is
locked in this
landscape's fierce

embrace as
the badger is whose
unappeasable jaws only

death unlocks from
the throat of rabbit
or rat and

moves, free yet
tethered, through
Time's inexorable weathers

in her solitary orbit
of the silent spaces
under the haunches

of her mountains and
the grey distended
udder of the sky.

A Snowy Good Friday

I take the snowy lakeside road today
past ice-frilled reeds that rustle in the sun
like cellophane; two stiff-necked whoopers eye
me from afar; the cold inflates a robin

on a white-capped stone and everywhere
the snow reveals the secret lives of men
and beasts: who would have thought, for instance, that
both fox and hare so much frequented this
bare place among the whins and rocks; that John
has twice already crossed this field today
with fodder from that haystack on his back
and stood, like me, under this overhang
to watch his steaming Friesians eat their fill
of hay that once was grass and flowers rooted
in the earth beneath their feet; who would have thought
that I was not the first to bowl pine cones
across the frozen shallows of the lake
and pit the drum-tight ice with fusillades
of stones like any vandal tempted by
a pane of glass?
                        The boles of trees and poles
and fencing posts are piped with ermine down
one side and sheep I thought last week were white
stand dazed and lost in dazzling drifts of light
as if bewildered by a landscape that
they thought they knew until it changed itself
into something as utterly strange and
new as that commonplace threadbare scrap
of daylight moon up there does night after night.
A wisp of wild geese in the distance fades
like wind-blown smoke; the woods are full of small
mysterious sounds as snow that fell
as silently as light now melts in tears
it sheds for Him whose death it mourned in white.

Blessings

Yesterday, for some reason I couldn't
understand, I suddenly felt starved
of trees and had to make tracks towards
the beeches of Lough Eske to set my heart
at ease and stand there slowly adjusting
myself to the overwhelming presence of all
those trees. It was like coming back among
people again after living for ages
alone and as I reached out and laid my
right hand in blessing on the trunk
of a beech that had the solidity but not
the coldness of stone I knew it for
the living thing it was under the palm
of my hand as surely as I know the living
sensuousness of flesh and bone and my
blessing was returned a hundredfold
before it was time for me to go home.

The Sinner And The Snow In The Glen

The first crocuses are
candle flames among
the starched altar-cloths
of late snow; the gate pier's

surpliced; under
a crucifix of weeping ice
nunneries of snow-
drops bow their heads,

pendulous and heavy
as thuribles; blood-red,
huge, the sanctuary
lamp hangs over Carn

on a faint chain of stars;
white inviolate aisles
creak under my feet
and the weight of my sins.

On Leahan

Another year has gone by since we heard the voices.
Innocence grows harder and harder to find
and death has taken its customary toll.
You have acquired your first grey hair.
Today as I climb the mountain in drifts of rain
the sea sends up its smoke-signals among the rocks,
the season for orchids has long since passed
and the ferns in the scree have begun to turn
into traceries of rusted wrought-iron filigree.
Points of mercurial light dance on the horizon.
I remember how on the summit that day
we heard the voices of playing children calling
out to one another in a language neither of us
had ever heard before and may never hear again.
We searched and searched but found no one:
not even the print of minuscule feet
in the soft black rain-pitted peat. Then the voices
faded away.

I have come here alone today to listen
once more but I have heard nothing except
the song of the wind in the rib-cage of a dead sheep,
the crying of curlews in the rain,
and now in the pub hours afterwards a man
tells me of someone who claims to have heard
the same voices we heard that day.
He speaks in a serious matter-of-fact way
like someone discussing the price of houses or cars.
I know I'll come back. Again and again. I might even
try to pick up some of the language.

A Roofless Cottage near the Horse Glen
at Twilight

It was not my tears that watered the weeds in the hearth
and pocked the earthen floor;
only the clouds that grieve for the sun
weep for them any more.

It was not my hand that razed the chimney to the ground
and bushed the gap of the door;
only the wind that grieves for the void
laments them any more.

It is not my voice, nor the wind's or rain's, that you hear
in the room Neil pens his sheep;
only the voices of nameless doomed lovers
whispering endearments in their sleep.

The New Scholars

Their fathers tramped the length of the glen
to school. In sun sometimes but mostly in rain.
Their fathers tramped it barefoot, hungry.
They take the bus to a school in town.

Their fathers and *their* fathers learned to count,
to read and write: that was enough for them.
They had no eye for the light on high ground,
could see enough with the light in the glen.

But the new scholars, their wind-washed eyes on
the horizon beyond the lip of the glen,
stare up towards the sheep on high ground and
the light their fathers found too dazzling for them.

Undine And The Seal

for Anthony Glavin

He treads water to get
a better view of you:
the bald wet

dogshead gleams like
sunlit wrack: the eyes
are soulful

as my bitch's but
I know it is a bull—
the thick fat

neck of him; the bulge
of that brutal profile—rising
up to watch the wind

lick your body into shape:
cleft of bivalve, soft-
shelled limpets

of your breasts, the caves
Love will as surely fathom
as this seal

fathoms the cavernous
mysteries of the sea
again and again.

A Little Thing

She married late: an islandman who reeked
of fish and turfsmoke; the sea was on his
lips and in his kisses. She liked that
and in bed at night she liked listening to the way
the Gaelic suddenly came spurting
out of him the same time as his seed. A little
thing she missed: the trees of home, evenings
of splintered light, a net of shadows tangling
and untangling on the grass. He said
that she was mad, that others had tried and failed,
but she went on and now she has this stump
of hawthorn and a stunted sycamore
too low to ever tangle with the light.

Nothing will coax an inch more out of them.
She hates their sickly look. He laughs.
I told you so. A tree will never grow out here.
And kisses her to sweeten what he says.
She tastes the bitterness of salt.

In Memory Of Patrick Boyle 1905—1982

It was snowing in Glenveagh the day you
died, Moylenanav was white, and the red
deer watched us through fluted curtains of flowered
light; the torrents were writhing like serpents
in the heather and the waterfalls hung
out of the sky like the entrails of clouds;
the wind was skinning the boles of birches
and peeling the scabs of lichen
from the scalps of the stones and we were cold
that day as we ate our brown bread and cheese
under a dripping rhododendron
but not as cold as you were, Patrick Boyle, had
we known it then, laid out on your bed
on the far side of Ireland.
                                        The deer turned their
beautiful buff-coloured rumps
into the wind and one stag with antlers twisting
out of its head like a thorn bush
out of a split crag paused for a moment to stare
at us out of eyes as impenetrable
and mysterious as the wilderness
in which it was bred.
                                I remembered those
eyes when they told me, Patrick Boyle, that you

were dead and how you looked at me that last
time I saw you alive with the eyes
of a stag being hunted towards the ultimate
wilderness for which we are all bred.

A Soft Day

Myself and the dog. A thorn
that in autumn's all scarlet with haws now
shining with pendulous tear-shaped drops,
faint prints of wind on the pane of the lake,
the sea, crouched low in its lair on the
horizon, growling, baring its teeth, and,
far off on the side of a hill last night's
heavy rain has criss-crossed with the links of
a broken white chain, the wake of a hare
rising like smoke from long wet grass.
The applause of pigeons bursting out of the ash.

Wittgenstein

For years, deciding that he knew it all,
he switched to simpler, less demanding arts
until, discovering that he might be wrong,
he found that language determines how things are,
an element, not a precision tool,
something mind inhabits, a bird in air,

the fish of logic in a verbal pool,
and, boring some student from his wooden chair,
did he make him wonder if, alone in rooms
or silent for hours with Russell thinking
of sin and logic, there might not be *someone* who,
like Carmen or Betty, transcending
the limits of logic, reason, art,
could teach him the private language of the heart?

The Young Curate

He lived alone till she arrived and she
is one of them: a sheepman's widow
without child, soft and shapeless as a ewe
at shearing, her tongue barbed as one
of their fences. In the flagged kitchen at night
he hears their sing-song voices—English
uneasily riding the Gaelic undertow—
often the low growl of a dog.
He sees them sometimes silently filing
along the gravelled path towards
the kitchen door like sheep along
a mountain track. She feeds him well but leaves
him to himself: this is a world of men,
dogs and women come when summoned.
A sick call and she's up and out before
him to the hall and gossiping with
someone—as if death too could wait like
this man standing, cap in hand, inside
the door. In time he will grow used
to almost everything—the solitude,
the sparsity of trees, the reek of turfsmoke

from his clothes—everything except the way,
perfumed and fur-coated for the weekly
shopping trip to town, she settles
herself into the front seat of his car
like a clocking hen on a clutch of eggs.

Condy At Eighty

Going to sleep at night sometimes he
imagines he hears the cries
of young girls but wakes at dawn

to the bleating of sheep in the rain.
The wind has spared one sycamore but
each year sap still rises in it;

in summer it holds out the palms
of its hands to a miserly sun.
When he prays or swears the words

come in Irish: roots are the last
to die. If he had ever made love
the words would have come that way

too. The silence of the glen is
the silence at the bottom
of the sea; he has been drowning in it

for as long as he can remember:
a slow death. No one
understands his cries for help: it

46

is a private language he shares
with God and his dogs. The beds
of the torrents are paved with broken

stones from the heart of the mountain
and the light breaks loose from the clouds
like a wild thing; soon it is trapped

in shadows. In eight years these
granite hills can break a working
dog. It took longer to break him.

Revelation

I hardly knew him: I was only six.
And photographs don't tell you much: we put
masks on for them, learn certain facial tricks.
I caught his smell once in a mouldy suit

but how to disentangle truth from lies
is harder than evoking things by smell.
I can't forget what happened to her eyes
one Christmas night when she began to tell

me how they'd run away from home, and stopped.
It was enough: no need of anyone,
of snaps or odours then: this lean close-cropped
man was suddenly a hero to his son

and she a heroine, love's mystery
a torrent glimpsed from flat lands by the sea.

Going Under

Maybe the bishop thought he had the stuff
of sainthood in him. Like that holy man
whose rude stone hut still stands beside the pier.
He should have known better: bodies or souls
don't dry out here; he'd have gone mad without it.

Now, the island fast going under, listing
like a ship about to founder, each night,
terrified beyond reason, he lurched about

that tilting deliquescent deck until,
feeling the final convulsive shudders,
drunken lumps of it bowling him over,

he jumped and surfaced somewhere in Europe
with just a single island souvenir:
a listing ship trapped in a whiskey bottle.

The Writing Room

So much of his life was spent in this room
full of books, this mortuary for a heart
and mind embalmed, this sparsely-furnished tomb,
where, sounding the shallows and the depths, he charts

the wrecks of love silted up in marriage.
Nothing ever *happened* in this room.
What happened happened elsewhere in a rage
of love and hate: in the tiled kitchen's gloom

where the cat curled up at the fire or a bee
trapped in a web indifferently eyed
another fire blaze as she and he
watched on TV how love was born and died.

Or in that red-carpeted upstairs room
where no one saw them shaping up to doom.

Letting Go

for Gerard Moriarty

He came today to take away her things
(I'm glad I wasn't there to see them go):
blouses and dresses, lingerie and rings,
even that tattered doll minus its toe.

I know we have to let them live their lives.
Not even love can change a thing like that.
Live and let live it was and it survived
the dramas of her love life and her hats.

But something deeper warns us to let go,
one of those things we never put in words.
Out of the darkness sunlit flowers grow,
under the silken cloak scabbards and swords.

Lives are for living: she must live her own.
The mystery of love is flesh and bone.

Blue

There's someone burning scrub down by the lake.
We smell the tang of it among the trees
and hear the crackle and the spit before
we glimpse blue smoke thinning in the breeze.

I wish I knew why things like woodsmoke
stir you so; I wish I knew the reason why
I am always losing you, as I lose
you suddenly now, to the blue of the sky

and the blue Bord Fáilte mountain in the lake
and all the blue translucencies of smoke
that dream such dreams of blueness in your eyes
you would not waken even if I spoke.

Death

We climbed all day through inundations
and inundations of light until
the islands shrank

in size to stepping stones across a burn.
Cloud shadows broke wild as March hares over
the screes; thick wet

lips of peat bared the stones of their teeth
at us; the wind combed partings white as bone
in your hair.

And then I saw the falcon fall from the sky:
arc after dark arc slicing the incandescent light;
I held my breath.

He nearly took you once: your grazed face
white as a tooth or a bone under
that fierce stoop.

The Island Cow

has the unhurried gait of
a barefooted woman balancing
a gourd of water

on her head. You know she
will never spill as much
as a single drop

of last night's dew from
her back nor tread on
a lark's nest

in the long grass. Her pace
is the pace of the tides,
full moons becalmed

in cloudless skies, scythes
in the stone-walled meadows.
Around the peg

of her tether through the field
of her gravity she moves at
the pace of the seasons.

The Hairs of Her Head

for my brother, Michael

The nuns had cut her hair the day before
and now these outraged eyes in a white cropped
felon's head that scarcely dents the pillow bored
like gimlets into mine. *You* should have stopped

them doing this to me is what they said,
and said until she died—as if aware,
like Samson, of all the strength that
lay in the glory of her much-cherished hair

that was waist-long that childhood day she was
drowning in the Erne and black as her boots
as her sister grabbed and held on though she could see
strands of it snapping close to the roots.

All that's left of it now is upstairs, locked,
with her trinkets and things, in a box.

The Ashplant

For ages, buried in dusty bric-à-brac
and toys, it lay unnoticed in the lumber-
room until one night his tarmacadam
driveway rang with the thud of hooves and
heavy breathing sounds he hadn't heard
for thirty years. He ran outside and found this

52

bullock shying at its shadow on a wall
and four more lipping tulips on the lawn;
one roared and tossed its head in panic, sand-
wiched between the Escort and the Merc. He shooed
and semaphored, shouted and shook his pipe
at them, but they ignored this dervish
in his pin-stripe suit until suddenly he
thought of it and rushed inside and dug
it from its grave and, facing them across
a bed of trampled flowers and waving it,
he felt the magic come and watched them melt
back into the darkness where a barefoot boy
is standing near a wizened little man
in torn serge trousers and a knitted cap,
an ashplant like a sceptre in his hand
and at his back the kingdom of bog and rock
his son had flogged to German millionaires
before he was cold in Malin sand and stone.

Addict

Look, they say in the glen, is something wrong
that he's taking that old hill-road again,
I wonder what he thinks of all day long?

Look, the bogmen say, lost in the heather,
has he nothing better to do with his time
than take to the hills in *this* kind of weather?

Look, the forestry workers say, that's him
up there on that spink beyond the tree-line,
if he doesn't take care he'll break a limb.

Look, the sheepmen say, watching him throw
yet another stone on the summit cairn,
thon man's as light in the head as a sick ewe.

Look, they all say, look, will you tell me why
when he turns his head to the hills, there are
shadows like clouds in the blue of his eye?

Weathers

Slieve League's marbled with February snow
but larks are warming up here at its base.
Waves of unreal light break over sheep and cows.
The sea's white with acres of billowing lace.

The mountain inverts itself in the sky
in the lake, two different shades of blue.
A sea mist wears itself threadbare on stone.
Its lining of sky begins to show through.

You stride ahead into a cloud's shadow.
The dog's sniffing at some bones and feathers.
I follow. The way I have followed you
now for thirty years in all weathers.

John Clare

for Madge Herron

I am eye-level with harebells
and bees on a swelling curve
of the earth. The wind breathes
on the nape of my neck. I exchange
the integument of my body
for the pelt of the grass; beetles
and ladybirds inhabit the interstices
of my bones, explore the valves
of my heart. I insert my fingers
into the moist orifices of earth,
bruise my lips on clay and stones.
The swish of birds' wings brushes
against my ears like the silken
passage of girls in long dresses.
I enter the secret places
where worms turn the world
on their shoulders and pass the earth
through the alembic of their guts.
In the labyrinth of the green
forest I find them: a hare's foot,
horseshoes, a rainbow of lichen.
Someone calls me. The keeper comes,
trampling the light underfoot,
speaking a familiar language
I am trying to unlearn.
His words clash with the pealing
of birds, the tongued bells of flowers.

The Blue Boat

How do I know that the wrecked blue boat
asleep in the long grass under the alder
dreams it is whole again and still afloat?

Because when I passed it by one night last week
and the wind made a sudden stir in
the trees I heard the sound of timbers creak
and the swish of a keel in the lake.

from *The Boa Island Janus*

UPSTREAM

Identities

Fermanagh: half in and half out
of whatever its element is,
never quite sure at any time

whether it's one thing or the other,
land in water or water in land,
but amphibious like me amid

the fluencies and insularities that
lie even deeper than land or water and
host here in this graveyard by the lake

among the tussocked and hummocked graves
of Boa Island's Christian dead
to a squat twin-headed stone idol

that was looking two ways long before
I knew there were two ways of looking
upstream to a source and downstream to the sea.

Love Letters

H.M.H. The mustered consonants stand
to attention like soldiers on the page:
no surrender to the insidious
mellifluous importunities
of the songs the siren orchestrates
out of a, e, i, o, u. From the seduction
of vowels, Lord, deliver your consonants
and know your own by the sound of their names.

O'Shea, O'Flaherty, McHugh and McCool:
names that could hardly have been more than names
to him—not people they'd ever invite
to afternoon tea—until she came
vowelling like a swallow from the South
and melted every consonant in his mouth.

Icons

He used to lift me high above his head
like a football trophy until I was
eye-level with the cardboard print she'd nailed
above the fanlight in the hall. And when
I'd fall back into his arms, helpless with laughter,
and feel the sandpaper of his beard
against my cheek I'd suddenly smell
him and draw him deep down into my lungs

until I was drugged with love for him and
for the cobwebbed Christ I was too young to
understand my father must have thought such
a strange thing there. As strange as those pictures
of the King and Queen I used to see
in the houses of his people were to me.

Cancer

It was what I expected it would be
but for the smells: their rankness took my breath
away. They led me by the hand from cage
to cage. A monkey yawned and ate its fleas,
the reptiles slept, dreaming of sin and death,
a baby cried. I saw the lions and
the elephant and heard the parrots rage
all through that afternoon and felt a vague

mysterious sense of something going on
beyond what was going on here: a world I'd
sometimes glimpsed when for no reason at all
grown-ups would suddenly burst into tears
or kiss or, like my parents now, constantly
reach out to touch each other and touch me.

The Space Between

I used to help her make her bed that time.
I'd plump and pummel the bolster and pillows
back into shape again and smooth the rucks
and creases out of blankets and sheets
with the palms of my hands. I'd face her
with nothing between us but the ease of our
silence and the white lonely reaches she'd
now been abandoned to dream in alone

and I'd snap and billow the sheets until
I could feel the pulse and pull of her coming
through to me from the other end like love
trying to keep in touch when the lines
were still open and the space between us
no more than the width of a double bed.

The Language Bog

You learned to pick your steps from stone to stone:
one false move and you could get bogged down
in what for you was treacherous ground you were
only beginning to find your way through
by circuitous routes and in disguise.
You were barefooted and unsure but they
knew exactly where they were going and,
dryshod, kept passing you out on the way.

We kept them to ourselves: contraband
it could be dangerous to declare: those words
we took out like love letters or keepsakes
when we were alone or with our kin,
confession, benediction, chapel, nun,
sure-footed now as sheep on their own ground.

The Language of Flowers

I bought my first one from a man I knew
and wore it like a wound in my lapel
but wondered why the boys who made a rush
towards the door before *God Save the King*
would never pin a poppy to their chests.
And then I learned the language of flowers
and how you say the things you never say
by wearing a poppy on Remembrance Day.

In Belmore Street I wore my poppy for
the dead in war, for my father too and
his forebears and for my mother's mother
who came of that same stock. I wear it now
in memory of the Enniskillen dead.
The wounds *they* wore that day like poppies bled.

Faces

The subtleties are for the tribal eye.
What's in a face? the innocent might ask.
Nothing perhaps—except your life or death.
All through my God-dark childhood years I heard
the women's voices in the gathering
darkness of the other room whispering
like mourners at a funeral of what
they called the Protestant look and think

now of all those strange faces I saw
in family photographs: Tuttles, Harveys
I never even met, and others who
somehow slipped away into the tribal night,
my father too, may he rest in peace, and
the long Protestant face of Louis MacNeice.

The Twelfth

We watched them come that day like an army
with banners to take possession of our
island town, tribesmen in tribal colours
waving flags, beating drums, planting their feet
in the loughside sheskins beside Ceithleann's
on her immemorial stamping ground.
You drew me close to you and sometimes ran
your fingers through my hair. Even then

as we peered out at them through the lace-curtain mists
of our sitting-room window, uneasy
as wood kernes, I was learning to keep
my distance and learning history too
as I watched you breaking cover and showing
yourself at the window as they withdrew.

The Wheel Wright and the Boy

In memory of James Orr

Even then I thought of him as Joseph
the Worker ankle-deep in shavings
of oak and ash—as though he'd been snipping
curls from blond heads of crepitant hair all
day long and this was a barber's shop.
I saw the shape of the felloes in his stoop
at the bench, knots in the wood when effort
made the veins in his hands bunch and stand out.

I was a cross he had to bear: always
touching things and asking questions about
the icons of the maker: spokeshaves, awls,
planes, gouges, chisels, saws, all those names for
the mystery of love and how it works
even when it's working against the grain.

Limbo

I was too young to pay attention to
what maybe were the early warning signs:
the way he'd keep on endlessly stroking
his thinning hair with the palm of his hand,
inspect his face in a peeling blank wall,
break off in conversational midflight
to stare for ages at nothing at all,

so when he took to fishing in rat holes
with a long piece of string and a fish hook
baited with stale bread, it was years before
I could even begin to realise
the loneliness of a brother trapped in
the limbo he taught us was close to hell.

Foray

We went there first in force to sit a State
examination: enormous wrought-iron
gates, a sweep of gravelled avenue up which,
fearful of ambush, we straggled
towards a pillared classical facade. We glimpsed
their scouts and Byrne was for skirmishing
with some of them but settled in the end for
half-stifled tribal battle cries while I,

the bog-trotter always parting branches
beneath the castle keep to peer up
at faces I knew were vaguely like my own,
could not stop thinking of Ceithleann and
of melting back into the greenery of her
hedge school in the planting down the road.

Black

You were not black because your skin was black.
Colour was not a simple thing like that.
You could be whiter than a cenotaph
and still be black as night. Your colour was
something you *were*, like being fat or thin,
tall or small, and not the way you showed up
in the light of day. Scarlet your sins might be
but you were black because your soul was

black as the bags of coal Black Jack Carson
sold to his own from door to door. I heard her
whisper the words under the picture
of the Sacred Heart and charge them with the sort
of doom I saw yawning under the feet
of every Protestant colour-coded black.

Playing Games

You never played the other side but still
you played the game you knew they were playing
somewhere else on a better pitch. Crowds on
the sidelines cheered: they were playing the same
game as you. Every goal scored was own goal.
You never missed the missing players who,
everyone knew, kicked with the other foot.
They were saying the same thing about you.

I played two games. Perhaps that was easy
for me: I could wear colours I'd never
wear playing against the others 1 knew
would not be playing against me because
the hardest feat is not playing the game
but learning to kick the ball with both feet.

The Republican Reader

Night after night she'd read to me: stories
about Friar Tuck and Robin Hood.
I'd be all ears for what my ears were tuned
to hear, and yet at times I'd have a sense
of something more being in the sense of what
was in the words for her than was for me,
a sense of nuances I never even knew
were nuances eluding me, until

years afterwards at school and learning then
about the reigns of all their kings and queens,
their victories at Trafalgar and the Nile,
I'd think of her each time I read what she'd
call one of *them* and found what she'd call *us*
in small print at the bottom of a page.

DOWNSTREAM

Voyagers

Summers we went west to Donegal and
wonders: a farm between two waterfalls
in sight of mountains and the sea, the all-
night-long cacophony of corncrakes in
the meadow that was his pride and joy as
I'd set course for sleep by the open window.
The curtains would fill with wind like sails and
swish and billow until I'd feel I was

under way like a ship, and I was too,
I suppose, not like him lying next door
whose long voyage was drawing to a close
now and whose muffled laments would sometimes
reach me like a fogbound coaster calling
for a pilot at the mouth of the lough.

News of the World

Time had beached him like a stranded whale
on the bleak shores of a big brass bed. The past
sang to him: the sea in a shell. I
was his lookout at the window of the upstairs
room. He'd cup his hand round his ear
when I'd call out to him how many cows
Stinson was grazing on the long acre now.
I'd listen to news of a world he knew
long before I knew there was a world to know.

And so it would go on, with him left
high and dry and out of his element by the tide
and me all eyes for the eyes that always
seemed to be looking beyond me
at things I'd never be able to see.

The Myth Maker

The days of cattle-raiding dawn campaigns
to Connaught fairs were epics of the past;
he'd fallen amongst women now, and when
they'd leave me looking after him, and he'd
no more to say, we'd listen to the river
finding its voice down at the Falls. I liked
that and 1 liked the sense of being at ease

with someone who, resting at last from deeds,
disarmed, in bed, was equally at ease
with me as I shaped him into someone
as heroic and legendary as
Cathleen or Red Hugh who gave their names to
waterfalls they'd all be astonished now
to find no longer there to listen to.

The Seedbed

In memory of William Allingham

Even though it lay fallow for years now,
the big bed he found himself floundering through
these days knew all there was to know
about sowing seed. But she was years dead
and he, with the crop he'd once raised raising
crops of their own now, was well past planting
anything more than a word in your ear.
The right word at the right time it turned out

as seed he never even knew he'd sown,
or had it in him to sow, took root and
grew when he was long gone. I'm still
taking crop from the field. The one he tilled
for that townsman of his whose poetry
he used broadcast across the bed to me.

Trampcocks

All that day we were at trampcocks: winching
them up the listing seed-caulked deck
of the shifter until it shone like a polished
convent floor. Each trampcock left a perfect
circle suppurating like a wound in
the aftergrass, an underworld of crushed
anaemic stalks and stems, the clotted slimes
and juices of fecundity, seething
and heaving with the secret life I'd find

under stones or under the dark side of my soul
where the serpent, dreaming of love
like a seed in the earth dreaming of light,
was beginning to stir in the hotbed
of flesh I warmed in the fork of my thighs.

In The Meadow

We were standing a good bit apart
on the grass at the end of another day of

perfect weather. You were dressed for indoors
as you usually were and not for outside

and you looked a bit out-of-place and lost
as you always did in an open space—

even here in one of your father's fields.
We were watching them winching the last

of the trampcocks up the tilted deck of
the shifter but what we were really watching

was watching nothing at all. The cloud
shadows took ages to pass that day and

the tracks of the horse-drawn shifter shone like
ribbons of tinfoil in the crushed green plush

of the aftergrass and I don't have to tell
you what we were saying or what passed between us

because we said nothing and nothing at all
passed between us as we stood there a good bit

apart in a dream on the grass at the end
of another day of perfect weather

drawing closer and closer together.

The Lost Fathers

To reach the meadow field was just as much
as he could do that day, and there he'd stand
marooned among the archipelagoes
of shadow the copper beech cast on the grass.
I kept my distance—like a dog at heel.
We watched them turning swathes with wooden rakes.
Sometimes he'd wave his stick above his head
at distant figures crinkling in the pools

of rippling heat but no one ever hailed
him now or thought to come and rescue him.
And so, before the women missed him from
his high-backed chair, I'd sidle closer to
this castaway whose hand I wished would reach
for mine the way my father's used to do.

THE SEA

Glencolmcille Sunset

for Lawson Burch

A white cloud
shapes itself to the mountain
and smoulders. I think

of flamingos settling

or of Renoir's sensual women:
the pale pink-tinted
flesh a kiss will ignite.

The Daffodils

for Desmond MacAvock

You cut them dripping
wet and put them in
a vase

under the Vlaminck print
they breathed life into
the still-life into

the airless room laid out
with the corpses of so
many dead

things I could smell them
in the hall like
birth or

it was like the smell
Lazarus must have smelt
in the tomb

when life took him again
they were breathing
as quietly

as a sleeping child or
someone dying whose breath
will hardly

mist a glass they were
breathing but they were
breathing

their last bleeding
like severed
arteries

aching o aching
for the wholeness
of roots

the daffodils you bled
to death to make
a wound

of colour in this
airless room
their tomb

Legs

I met a sheepman and his three-legged dog
on Muckish today and stopped to ask him
why he'd tied its fourth leg up. He said it was
to slow him on the hill and when I wondered
if he'd ever let the dog
use its fourth leg again (I swear to God
I didn't blink an eye) he looked me up and down
from boots to beard, and smiling, said
he was just a pup but that he'd need it
when the time came—like some people need sticks
and fixed me with two eyes as blue and as
inscrutable as the sky overhead
before I went my solitary way

(around a cairn as massive as a house)
reflecting that a dog, even a dog
like this leading a dog's life, might indeed
be better off than me when I'm too old
to climb mountains without, as the sheepman
said, the services of an extra leg.

Heron

In memory of Beatrice Behan

was assembled out of bits and scraps, not made.
Like one of those early flying machines held together
          with glue and twine.
His undercarriage is an afterthought sticking out behind.
He is all wings and no fuselage and probably hollow inside.
Finn could have blown him off the palm of his hand.

He creaks into flight. The wind buffets him, gives him
a bumpy ride: it seems he must somehow end up
in a twisted heap of canvas and struts on the mountainside.
But no: he tacks into weathers with a prow that rises
          and falls in the swell.
The ghost of the pterodactyl haunts him in every cell.

He alights: furls his wings like a wet umbrella, settles,
          rapt and murderous,
drying out in the wind and sun on the edge of a tarn
or hunched over a pool in the burn pretending he's
a blind one-legged beggarman or a mystic
          communing with God.
Too late, too late for the fish or frog when it realises
          he's not an old cod.

Heron invented slow motion long before the movies came but
allows himself the lightning of his pickaxe
          for the killing game.
Heron's the icon of the silences beyond the last tongues
of land where the islands float and quiver like mirages
          in the light,
he's the hermit who daily petrifies himself in the reeds
          of the penitential lake,
the logo of the lonely places past the last sheep and
          the last house,
the El Greco or Modigliani doodle in a remote corner
          of the evening sky where
the newsprint of distant waders swims before the eye,
heron's that sudden outlandish screech you hear at midnight
in the water meadows as he changes into the wrong gear.

Diaspora

for Nik Cohn

Out of a leaden sky at dawn
the falcon falls
all talons on its prey
and under it
everywhere
in death's hushed air
islands
laid out like corpses
in their shrouds of mist.

The Road to the Lighthouse

Unteased wisps of
sheepswool mist
pricked on outcrops
of rock; the scent
of wet scythed grass
on sea air; spilt
light awash on
island and field; land
stripped to its bare
bones as a lone
man, lean as a bent
thorn, intent as a hawk,
on a sunlit headland scans
the sea with cupped
hands for his lost sons.

Mysteries

Who laid that timber plank across the burn
and hacked a path straight through the hazel scrub;
who sank a water butt beyond the turn
where whins take Cormac's tractor to the hub;

who fenced that sheep-run high above the screes
and hung the gate that wasn't there last night;
whose axe wreaked havoc in the lakeside trees;
who limed the gable such a dazzling white;

whose plough re-textured greycord into brown;
who trimmed the hawthorn hedge down to the quick;
who dressed the turf-stack in a see-through gown
and put a hair-net on the bee-hive rick?

I marvel at what happens when I turn
my back on townlands that I lately trod.
The hands of men work as secretly and
mysteriously as the hand of God.

The New Gap

One time I'd have said that wood had little
chance against stone. Until I noticed what

a growing tree did to Patrick's wall I'd
have said that wood was much like flesh and bone

and stood no chance when it came up against
stone, but I was wrong and now where Patrick's

drystone wall once bulged with a belly not
unlike his own there's a new gap for ewes

and lambs that wouldn't be there at all if
wood had stood such a poor chance against stone.

Love in the Glen

Never having paraded their love
in the public sense of interlinking hands
and exchanging kisses on the street but
being private in their affections as in
their lives, now that they've grown older and
some of their passion's spent, they compensate
for what they've lost by holding hands in bed.

Touch: In The Demountable

I notice now they seldom shake your hand—
not even if they're going for plane or boat.
I miss that Sunday trip to second Mass.
I shook more hands than Neil did for the vote.

I used to pat the children on the head,
invite them in for sweeties and a chat,
but things are not the same and now they'd be
suspicious of a simple thing like that.

Sometimes I think a lot about the past:
my mother used to squeeze me till it hurt;
I wrestled with my father on the grass
and made it with a girl one night at Burt.

They took me once to hospital in Carn:
a stoon of pain: och, nothing very much.
I cried the night they left me back at home:
thon blondie lassie had a gentle touch.

I never married; all my kin are dead.
A week ago I had some swollen glands
and grabbed the doctor's thumb to say good-bye.
The new-type curate calls but won't shake hands.

Brian's House

The glen was full of barking dogs but you
kept none: you'd sold out to the forestry
years ago and had no need of one, and so
in time the hill behind your house has
darkened with trees and the shadows of trees
and your old stamping ground, where you ran
a few score of black-face ewes until
arthritis tethered you to the half-circle
round your front door, now nourishes nothing
but the roots of conifers. Last week
on a day as warm as that summer's day
the two of us sat on the drystone wall
outside your door chatting for ages about
how some things in life go right, some wrong,
and how so much that was good has now gone,
last week I came that way again past
the barking dogs and the wind-scoured farms
of the people of the glen and past the house
that once had no dog and now has no man.

Spring At Murvagh

Although the mountains are still seamed with snow
and, a moment ago, fusillades of hail
were beating on the corrugated tin roof
of the shed, and the trees are bare,
I sensed something indefinable
here today that was not here yesterday:
the way, in a room where nothing much
is happening except maybe for a woman
staring out the window at cows
and a man reading a book by the fire
in a chair, you suddenly sense the presence
of love like a fragrance in the air.

Theorem

for Johnny Boyle

The smallest field in West Donegal,
half-way between Glenties and Dungloe,
has fine drystone walls but no
gate; the biggest field in West
Donegal—not a stone's throw
away—has a splendid wooden gate but no
walls. I'm not sure what conclusion
I should draw from this—I pondered
the problem all the way to Loughanure—
except perhaps it's a theorem in wood
and stone to prove that a field in

Lettermacaward may be geometrically
defined as either a space with walls and
no gate or as a space with a gate and no walls.
One way or the other, I *know* what they think
of Euclid in Lettermacaward in West Donegal.

Sheepmen

The dog noses a steaming bag lumped
like an afterbirth at the open door.
Two kittens eye the *danse macabre*
of a leaf impaled on a thorn and the sky
is wet whitewash. God knows when it will dry.
What scarecrow's that an insidious wind
has stretched out on the broad of its back
in the furrowed reaches of the big brass bed?
Whose claws are those endlessly fondling
the folds of the bedclothes with a passion
never lavished on human flesh and bone?
Whose eyes are those that keep turning away from
the sparse light outside to the sparser light within?
Owen McSharry of Crieve is on his rack.
Today he waits for the priest to come creaking
up the narrow stairs past the hired woman
and the Sacred Heart picture on the wall
with the body of Christ in a box.
A sheepman like himself and the only one
he'd trust to rid him of this thing stuck
like a whinbush in the gap of his throat.

Stone

A good drystone wall knows where it stands
and, what's more, it knows what it is: it belongs.
It has character and strength and it wears
its years well: like a castle or a cathedral.
A well-built drystone wall fits itself
as snugly to the landscape as good homespun

does to a man; it rides the townlands like
a boat rides the swell; you can follow it
for miles and miles as it takes the rough
and the smooth in its stride. Certain drystone walls
have been there so long they are bone once more
of the landscape's bone rooted as much

in myth and history as a standing stone.
Sometimes they look like the land giving birth.
One drystone wall I know in Friary
is so fleeced with grass and cushioned with plush
tussocks of moss that you'd be hard put
to catch a glint of stone in it at all

and another I know in Greenans is
so threadbare you can see sky showing through.
In Lough Eske Wood there's a tumble-down
straggle of stones masquerading as wall
through which impudent wrens flicker like tongues
of shadow and stoats thread their sinuous way

and, on a day of rainbows and cloud shadows
you can glimpse something more like
spittle than showers fleetingly speckle
the walls of Ardnamona until you think

it's a new grain in the stone you hadn't
noticed before or instant weathering.

I know there are people round here who think
I'm a bit gone in the head the way
I keep going on about drystone walls but
I could go on for as long, or longer,
about old houses, castles, cathedrals.
What I'm gone in the head about is stone.

Setback For Spring At Lough Eske

A lean East wind flays
the skin of the lake into
livid streaks and thin
March sunshine affords
no comfort to the man
whose bill-hook methodically gashes
the limbs of the hedge with
ivory wounds; while out at the edge
of the reeds under a sky
as cold and hard as porcelain
a swan up-ends its immaculate
arse like a flag of surrender.

Cormorant

is wedded to the mysterious and enfolding
sensualities of the world of water and
shows off his sleekly-elegant conservative
designer-class good looks among flotillas
of unseaworthy-looking gulls riding the swells
like floats or children's celluloid ducks;

sits low in the currents and rips like
a submarine with her decks awash and
when he's partly hidden from view in a trough
watches you suspiciously over the top of a crest
through the constantly-swivelling periscope of his
now fully-extended s-bend of a neck;

leads a Jekyll-and-Hyde double life and,
a split second before he submerges
to assume the identity of a multiple killer
in the Victorian murk of the groundsea
underworld of the sound, he decapitates
himself like a swan and, surfacing again and

nervously alert and bobbing about like
a featherweight in a first-round bout, with all
his systems geared for instant action, he fixes
you in his sights before you've even had
time to pick him out in a welter of water
and light but shows his true colours when

he unfurls his wings like a swastika on the rocks
to flaunt them at the frigate's union jack.

Fern

is a copycat arching its back
under the half-hoops of the bramble and, later,
a small child's minuscule bunch-of-bananas hand;
is the crozier of a bishop or
a Viking longship dragon,
the isosceles triangle of isosceles triangles,
a measure of the wind's weight in calm weather;
is a fish picked clean to its green bone,
a bonsai Christmas tree pressed paper-thin,
the groundling's answer to the freedom of the feather,
the wing of a malingering plover
or a Gothic window grille of rusted metal;
is osteoporosis of the bracken
whose boneyards I crackle through and
whose ghosts begin to haunt window panes
in the first hard frosts of late autumn.

Storm Petrel

has spent a lifetime trying to perfect
the technique of being able to walk

on water. He scans the surface of the sea
myopically and keeps dipping his feet

in the waves to test them for the exact
temperature at which faith once sustained

the weight of Peter's body on the Sea
of Galilee forgetting that faith is not

an acquired technique in his unremitting
efforts to live up to a famous name.

Magpies

might have once been part of some fabulous
operetta irretrievably lost
in transit and now whirring raucously

about our dazzling sets and backdrops
like wound-up mechanical props on the loose
and about to run out of power but

there's nothing operatic about them when,
hopping mad on the road round splatters
of squashed guts and bones, they pick the tarmac

clean again or when a lone one crosses
the path of Mary Bridget on her way
to the well and stops her dead in her tracks.

Ravens

never had a good press, infesting
old lays and legends long after
they'd finished off Chuchulain like
daylight Transylvanian bats or
transmogrified witches, two black
hags flapping heavily about the glens
day after day cracking their gallows
jokes, trailing a sick lamb or
a stricken fox, picking the eyes out
of the living and the dead. Only
last week I saw a pair shadowing
an old man out after sheep on Suhill.
Pity poor Con the undertaker
if they took a fancy to him.
Ravens are real eye-openers.

Picking Mushrooms

Look how they break in your hands like soft chalk or
sacramentally like bread, how sometimes you come
on one the accordion-pleated beams of whose cupola

are enclosed with a thin white membrane and
how if you should happen to put your finger
or your thumb through this gossamer skin

you are suddenly overcome with the sense of
having violated the perfection
of God's handiwork the way it is when

you mar the cloud-crowded radiance
of a beach just glazed by the tide or
a starched sheet of virgin snow

with the print of your feet or
the way it was for a moment once when
the veil of the temple of her body was rent.

Funeral

Interminable slaughter and
crippled lives, tribes
and the barbed language of tribes,
Norseman and Norman,
Planter and Gael,
and the terrible incubus,
history, riding the present,
whispering lies. What more pitiful
than to hear them begging
their God for mercy yet again
under these cold Northern skies?
Look how the closed faces
mirror the closed minds
of the past's masters, setting
hate at the throat
of love even at the edge
of the grave, promising
apotheosis to all in exchange
for the ritual blood sacrifice,
drawing the sting out of death
with moth-eaten battle cries. And this
has gone on for centuries, centuries.

The Magic Realists

Tonight, all over this divided city
where people in small terraced houses
are viewing the big gangster movie on BBC,
one family, watching a mobster
riding shot-gun in a stolen car, hears him
come raging through their own front door.

Vulture

A sheepman in the Mournes observed it first
gorging on the entrails of a still-born
lamb; next it was disturbed plucking the heart
from an aborted human foetus unborn

for better things elsewhere and on the third
day poachers stoned it from the corpse of an
informer they found gagged with a dragon's turd
and testicles. But it grew weary on
such rich fare, scavenging the abattoirs
of hate until, enormous, gross, and fat
with the viscera of the dove and rat,

sated yet home-sick for the heat and flies,
it bore South again, smelling a sweeter war
where God died long ago of tribal lies.

Referendum

That big drunken man over there
with the twisted mouth starting to sing
Sean South in a tuneless voice,
is that the sheepman whose son was shot?
Aye, that's him. Nahor Devenney of Crieve
a stroke felled on the side of his own hill
and left lying half a December night that took
the last grain of sweetness out of him.
A hard man. In this very pub the day
before the vote he turned his cold eye on me
and said out of the corner of his crooked
mouth that it was a clean thing to kill Brits
with guns but that he'd take a horsewhip
to any son of his he caught with a condom.

Cargoes

Tory of the waves: of warrior and
saint : Balor's island
and Colmcille's,

swathed in seamist, lists under
its weight of myth and
history : Tau

cross and Fomorian fortress, cursing
stone and round tower, shades
of the Norse

marauders forever riding
the fierce white dragons
of the sound.

A rat will not live on Tory island: on
Colmcille's holy ground : but I
look over

at Ireland : insular too, another
ship listing under its own
constantly-shifting

lethal cargo of myth and history, full of
laughing boys, wood kernes, priests, the rats
in the hold

nosing and sniffing at the corpses of all
the grand warriors
and saints.

Fishermen

for Derek Hill

Who's that dour man with the quarried face and
the gnarled hands lumped in his lap like turnips?
Him? That's Nahor in from the island with
the salmon from last night's big run. Now he's
filling his gut before he goes back out.
Look at the eye of him. Try and plumb it.
Cast your net in him. What'll come up in it?

A decapitated cross, a cursing stone,
the broken images of older gods, shards of
obscure Gaelic. Splash him with God's holy water
and it runs off him like rain off an upturned currach.
The saint was out there once fishing for men?
When he trawled so wide he should've trawled deeper.

Museum Piece

Somehow the tumbling paddy always took
my fancy most when we were at the hay.
I'm not sure why. Maybe it was the name,
that hint of clownishness, or the awkward
lumbering elephantine way it broke
with gravity, that drew me to this huge
horse-drawn wheelless wooden rake whose cartwheels
through the meadow I'd want to emulate.

But that was years ago and here today
among the traps and carts, the creels and churns,
I know my place and stand now not beside
the tumbling paddy dreaming of take-off
but like another effigy beside
the immemorially earthbound plough.

The Black Sheep

Listen. The Angelus bell has begun
to toll faintly in the glen. And look,
over there under a low sky bloated with rain,
a man mending fences who takes off his cap
to no one but God and to eat and sleep,
has suddenly bared his head to pray.
Two dogs lie prostrate like acolytes at his feet.
I know his name and the names of his dogs and
once I broke bread with him in the kitchen
of a womanless house as bare and white
as the limewashed house of his God down the road.
We talked about ewes and wethers and how
he'd been searching for a black sheep he'd lost.
I remember the coil of rusted barbed wire
sitting on the bald skull of a boulder like
a crown of thorns encrusted with dried blood
and the ragged cross on the side of his hill
was the skeleton of a flayed scarecrow marking
the place where a crop had failed and he gave in.
And I remember too how he and his dogs
penned me in a corner of that windswept
kitchen like a sheep that had strayed from
the fold of the crucified Sheepman hanging
like a scarecrow from a nail in the wall.

Lovers

You went there first with us one April day.
Remember? The sky was what Yeats used call

dove-grey and we took you by the hand among
the trees. There was a smell of resin on

the wind and daffodils among the whins,
and bees. And now you say your lover took

you there today. So, tell me all about
the colour of the sky and whether all

the birch boles that were red when we were there
have turned a silver grey. And what about

the resin on the wind and all those
daffodils among the whins, the bees?

You hadn't time to take in everything!
Tell me, did you even *see* the trees?

Firsts

for Attracta

I found your mother there and pine martens
in the bens and two basking sharks like cloud
shadows darkening the bay. The busman

arrived at our door one day bristling with
the antennae of a live lobster and
a corncrake clattered away all night long
under our window in the wilderness
of rank grass we called a lawn. They were all

firsts for me and so was the swallow I
saw the following year flashing over
a half door to the nest I knew was cupped
close up against the beam of the roof
like a stoup for the holy water the priest
scooped up into his hand to baptise you.

The Measure

for Nancy McHugh Yates

There's hardly a better way of doing
nothing than sitting on a Lough Eske wall
speckled with green and orange lichens and
overshadowed by foxgloves four feet tall.

Even better is to teach your children
this art of doing nothing at all
by making them sit at the lake beside
you on top of a lichened drystone wall.

And after all that they'll probably leave
you sitting alone on your Lough Eske wall
with nothing except foxgloves to show you
what they were like when they were four feet tall.

Words And Music

Even though you're still afraid of horses
and cows I know now, by the way you fill
your jeans and blouse, this doesn't mean you'll take
to your heels and run at the sight of boys. Look
how the sheen of an orange-tip's wing shines
in your hair and, daughter, tall and wind-blown
as that pendulous foxglove by the drystone wall
that needs a bra more urgently than you,
I notice how your eyes change colour
in the light like the distant lake-water
I glimpse through the trees—something surely for
someone, apart from your mother and me,
to dream about now. Who would have thought
to look at you here as we stop by the sign
on the six-foot wall warning trespassers off
that once I watched your mother pat and
powder the small cracked moon of your bare ass
the way she kneads and flours dough to bake
bread or that I know a certain place more
secret and mysterious than even this
clearing in the woods where God when he made you
blew a dimple in your flesh as perfect
as one of those hollows blown here
last winter by the wind in snow? But
it's time to turn back: further than this
fathers, even fathers who are poets,
don't go, and so, my daughter, Orange-tip,
Foxglove, Snow, Lake-water, remember if
you in these woods should one day meet a boy
passionate but, unlike your father, tongue-tied,
tell him you know a poet who has words
for all the tunes that only he can play.

The Thunderstorm

for Danea

Your small hand, warm and vulnerable and
beautiful as a wild bird, slipped
out of the way of the storm into the sanctuary
of my hand. Into the nest of my flesh and blood.

Now, in your own time and season, out of the way
of the storm, in the sanctuary of your body,
in the nest of your flesh and blood,
you have cradled a child warm and
vulnerable and beautiful as a wild bird.

Fire

I went into you
like a pillar of singing fire
and sang in you until
you began to sing too and
then we were singing together
until we consumed each other
and the fire withdrew.

In me before you.

Mothwhite

Below us the sea's still stained with the spilt wine
of the sun but darkness is mopping
the last of it up. You are on a headland

out of sight. Above me on the terraces
of rock I smell the cows I cannot see,
hear their sighing and belching. And then

a sudden sound makes me look up from where
I'm standing to the headland and the sky.
You come ghosting towards me out of a night

warm and intimate as that over-heated
central-London room in which, years ago,
palpitant, mothwhite in the darkness,

someone I thought I knew was making strange with me
as I suddenly began making strange with her too.

The Song

Yes. I remember that day. Blue Stack was
a metallic white in the hard March light
and all the conifers were plumped with plumes
of snow. You were somewhere out of sight.

And then in a bare birch by the castle
wall a blackbird began to sing with such
wild passion that I suddenly knew in
my heart and nowhere else that it was Spring.

And sang until you came out of the trees
and we both stood listening to a song we
knew in our hearts and nowhere else has its
own seasons, and the bird sang on and on.

Knocknarea

It was on Knocknarea and there
was no one there but two young
lovers holding hands and this
middle-aged married pair.
A cloud of pollen from some
pines rose into the air like
fine snow and dusted your hair.
We marvelled at a pine cone's
colour and shape, the crusted
lichen on the megalithic stones.
The farms far below us were
toy farms and I wanted to
reach down and move the tiny
lead animals anywhere.
We climbed the cairn and
the lovers got lost somewhere
in the heather. We were
the middle-aged married pair and
the weather was Yeats country weather.

Planting And Felling

I hear the sound of felling in the glen
remembering how we often used make tracks
to plantings that they now are cutting down
with saw and axe.

We planted too, and it was done with ease,
but planting well's an art that may not last;
a dream of seedlings masting into trees:
all that is past.

I see the print of lovers crushed in grass—
was that a tear or raindrop in your eye?
No matter, dear, who bedded there, it was
not you and I.

Across the clearing sounds of felling peal
so loud and fierce we both stop in our tracks:
like burning ice cleaving my heart the steel
blade of an axe.

Protest

I came out of you, protesting, a long
time ago. You suffered but wept
with joy when you saw me, an eight-pound
boy. You would do it again, if you could,
to recapture that joy. I am
a man now, my few hairs are white, I have
acquired a paunch; I tower above you
who have shrunk like a fruit left too long
in the sun; every day we grow further
apart who once were one flesh.
You accuse me of neglecting you but
know I know that this is untrue. You
talk of the past as if it were yesterday
and complain of the ailments of age.
I have begun to talk like that too.
You weep in your room at night but
never again will you weep for joy.

Mother, I cried for you when they laid you
in the earth, I cried out against death as
I once cried out against birth when they took
me out of you, protesting, a long time ago.

from *Making Space*

Whales At St. John's Point

for Joan

It was all sea and sky out there that day.
It always is. You were with me and we
were in our element rediscovering
the elements of water, light, and air.
The skyline was hung with cobwebs of rain;
filaments of gossamer flashed in your hair.
Just another day looking at mountains,
clouds, flowers, until suddenly, abrim,

tidal with wonder, we saw the whales rise
up out of their element into ours.
Out of the mystery of water and myth
into light and air and into what would now
be a history indissolubly
part of the history of you and me.

The Song of Balor

for Moya Cannon

All night my fierce eye winks at the eye of the storm.
Give me *one* tree that the wind and sea can deform.

They have stripped me of flesh until I am skin and bone.
My voice is the grinding of seastone on seastone.

On reef after reef I bare my teeth at the clouds.
I spit at the sun trawling in shoals of shadows.

You hear more than the sound of the sea in *my* shells.
I have caves in my soul the saint never entered.

The Name

for Helen McHugh

Birra or Durnish: a lake near the beach
always white with tussocks of swans.
And one day last summer coming down
past the wooden sluice-gate with you—
the whirr of incoming wild duck,
a shimmer of waders far out at sea—
I found a white flower masting up through moss.
What's that? you asked. Grass of Parnassus, I said
and as soon as I said it the poem began in my head.
So I said it again. And again. Just the name.

Snow Again

The insect settled like an asterisk
on what I'd written since I rose at dawn
and then flew out through the open window
towards the small print of a bird. A footnote
to nothing on the white page of the lawn.

Primroses

We thought the whole world was at our feet then,
and most of the time it was I suppose.
We scrabbled in the wet mulch of roots
and were eye-level with ox-eye daisies
and lambs, picked the white pith out of elder
sticks the way we picked marrow out of bones
and ran barefoot across webs of moth-eaten
sand, but what we liked most of all, before

we grew away from that ground of wonder,
was finding windfalls in the long grass
of the orchard and in springtime eating
primroses the taste and texture of whose
petals I would instantly recall
on the lips of the first girl I ever kissed.

Mnemonic

I'll not easily forget Dunlewey today.
And neither will you. Not because
the sun shone on the mountains and the lake
and the first cuckoo was calling beyond
the hill and the whins were scenting the wind
from the scree; not because it was the first
warm day of spring and the blackthorn was
in blossom and the sycamore in bud
and wheatears were pirouetting on stones
and lambs bleating in the fields and people

109

sitting outside their houses enjoying
the good weather; not because of any
of these things will I remember Dunlewey
today but because, when we walked down towards
the glen together, we both kept talking
for miles and miles of someone we loved
and wishing she knew her way through the world
as surely as all the burns here know
their way to the lake through the heather.

Puffin

In memory of D.J. O'Sullivan

Puffin slipped out of the jungle aeons ago
and headed north to join the circus

when it came to town. That was easy for him
because he'd never forgotten how to paint his face

and he didn't have to act to act the clown.
Once he nearly brought the house down when he mistook

certain guyropes for the fattest sand-eels
he'd ever seen. Now he's a troglodyte

helping to raise his young in a hole in the ground.
When he's not doing that he's sitting sedately

among pin-cushion sea-pinks and shaggy rocks
on the edges of cliffs with thousand-foot drops.

Whatever you do don't put him in a cage
and think if you feed him nuts instead of fish

that he'll begin to scream "Bloody Hell!"
out of a corner of that multicoloured

neolithic axehead he calls a mouth
or rasp out other obscenities he must have picked up

down south from some foul-tongued first mate
of a buccaneer's ship in the Caribbean.

And then there's that walk. Is it a sailor's gait
or is he just camping it up? Puffin's a queer auk.

Death's Door

for Cathal Ó Searcaigh

Whatever it is, it's hardly the weather
keeps drawing me back to places like these:
a rock in the sea, a tarn in the sky,
a glen where nobody lives anymore
and where, if you shout there in English, you'll hear
the echo in Irish haunting your ear,
and, today, the side of a hill at the end
of a track—there was never a road—
near a bush and some broken-down walls
under a sky that's sagged so low
it's begun to snag on the cairn of the croagh.
I enter what's left of the roofless house

through the doorless doorway in the first spits of rain.
The jambs and the lintel have rotted away
and it's been open house here for lambs and ewes
since the night years ago the door was unhinged
to help the man of the house down his own
mountainside on the broad of his back.
I stand on the grass of the bedroom floor
waiting for the old whinbush to make
a sound I hear most times I come up here.
Listen. There it is. The creak of a door.

Bestiary

Nights and he empties himself of himself.
The dregs. All that's left of him now. What used
to wither away and die in the furrows of her flesh
now withers away and dies on the sheet
he didn't wash for weeks after she died.
He tents the bedclothes with his upraised knees,
lifts the edge of the coverlet and sheet,
but all he can smell is the reek of himself: bad seed.
You are different he hears the priest say,
you are not a pig or a cow or a sheep,
but remembers how they found the body
of Owney Ban curled up under a whinbush
like a beast that had crawled away
into a dark place to lie down and die.
He took her for granted. Like God or the rain.
Now all he can do is bury his head
in her clothes like one of his bitches
and sniff at armpits, crotches. Again and again.

Into the Depths

Up here on this sunlit headland lambs lie
in the hollows like tiny drifts of late snow.

I am sitting on a rock looking down
into the depths of the sea when I notice

something crossing the dunes with an airborne
float in tow. Something that's coming at speed

up a path on the face of the cliff.
Something I thought at first was a dog

that's stopping dead in its tracks at my feet
and is suddenly eye-to-eye with me

until I can see into the I of an eye
that never looked out of the eye of a dog.

I am sitting on a rock looking down
into the depths in the eyes of a fox.

Love And War

Beside this Ulster road flanked
with grass banks and summer flowers
the print of last night's lovers
brings the soldiers running running.

The Ring

It's gold. Engraved with her initials and a date.
She told me who he was and how that dream
of love had come to nothing in the end.
And why she wore it still and always would.
But love, that feeds, renews itself so much
on touch, on kisses and on hands, feeds
on love's memories too, has no beginning
and no end in human hearts, is always there
as it was there that summer day when she
plunged in to save a younger playmate who
was drowning in a pool below the Falls.
They're both long dead but I'm still here and I now wear
her ring. The ring I'd not be here to wear
if love had failed a drowning girl that day.
Love and those hands one of whose fingers wore
the ring my mother's sister used to wear.

The Scarecrow

In memory of Simone Weil

Sun, rain, snow, storm; the derision of crows;
God letting the world be what the world is;
the children of the children we fed
on a diet of stones with nothing
to throw at me now but the stones of their hearts.
Such weathers have reduced me to this:
a clown's trousers and a clawhammer coat,

my soul slowly beginning to leak
into the boghole at my feet. God knows when
the bliss of all this affliction will end
and the wind finally strip me of my rags
and lay me out on the ground in my shroud
of mist. Then you will know who I am and why
I wore the clothes of the creature called man.
I was made in the shape of a cross.

The Ghost in the Machine: A Haunting

ARMS AND THE MAN

I loved the sounds before I knew the sense:
Pax Domini sit semper vobiscum.
Surpliced and soutaned, kneeling at the foot
of the altar beside the sanctus bell
and sing-songing the responses, I thought
of a language of pure love reserved for God.
Then I read Virgil, who sang arms and the man
and who would never have heard tell of Him.

No more than that youth they've just discovered
dead might have heard tell of the poet whose
Aeneas gave his grandfather his name
and who took Dante on a guided tour
of Hell. They found his naked body, marked
with burns from an inferno, dumped on waste ground.

METAMORPHOSES

I helped to vest him in the sacristy
and now, the metamorphosis complete,
a bird of paradise had risen out
of the ashes of a crow. And surely
it was paradise he was catching glimpses of
behind closed eyes as I watched him withdraw
into the mystery of a world you
cannot enter with the world in your heart.

Hoc est enim corpus meum. He held
Christ's body between forefinger and thumb
but I was eye-level with two frayed black
trouser-ends and a pair of lumpish boots
and I could not stop thinking of the way
the world is bread and wine and feet of clay.

GOOD FRIDAY

Love in abeyance. Godforsakenness.
Ships of the soul stricken, foundering fast;
the statues shrouded, the altar stripped,
the doors of the tenantless tabernacle
thrown wide open and the church suddenly
bare and Protestant as an unfurnished
room in an unoccupied house with me
praying for the old tenant to return

and for love too and the lights of candles,
an altar fragrant again with spring flowers,
the mystery of veils, closed golden doors,
and the joy of glimpsing the risen Christ
coming down the aisle to show Simon Peter
the prints of the nails in his hands and feet.

THE DARKNESS

Pride, covetousness, lust, gluttony, envy,
anger and sloth: I knew they were all sins
but when I opened the door into the darkness
of the confessional I was in the dark
about most of them. Except the one
that slept coiled up in the darkness of flesh
and would not let my soul burst into flower
again until he'd absolved me and the world

was suddenly light, wonder, Chagall and Blake,
was towers of ivory, houses of gold,
and I was breaking out of the field
of sin's gravity and, buoyant with joy,
afloat in space like a levitating saint
on the terrible thermal of God's grace.

THE MISSION

They had one-track minds and declamatory hands;
they were superb actors in a dying
histrionic tradition not unaware
of the dramatic impact of a black
biretta flourished above a bowed head.
They strode like soldiers into embattled
pulpits and wore crucifixes like swords
at their waists. Their invocations were

trumpet calls to battle against the world
the flesh and the devil and the candle
in my hands could have been a faggot lit
to burn another heretic. They flushed
sin from the coverts of my soul with fear.
Where was love hiding if it wasn't here?

117

INCUBUS

I lay sleepless. The room was dark as sin.
Nothing astir outside or in except
the mind of God that never rests and mine
bestraddled by the incubus of thought
that some nights rides from hell. Once, heaven stood
by this bed, invincibly it seemed, but now
was only fear of death: the mystery no one
solves or fails to solve without at first being dead.

What could I set against the dark except
that I was still haunted by a ghost
in a machine? The son of God, never
so much himself as on the cross, cried out:
My God, my God, why have you forsaken me?
Who speaks his mind when his heart's in his mouth?

THE BOOK

I turned over my soul. It wasn't there.
I found an angel embattled under the sin
of lust. Its wings were bespattered and it
was gasping for breath in the foetid air.
So I sat outside the walls of the city
and waited for someone to come with bells
ringing and singing to open the narrow gate
and welcome me back in. And no one did.

And so I learned how to live alone
in the desert of matter and dream
of the book that's kept for registering
sparrows, hairs of the head, even the creatures
that crawl out from under atoms and spit: *Where
do you think you'll find your name indexed there?*

Hail and Farewell

The big bull calf, all sea legs after nine
months afloat, was in his element now,
gorging himself less on milk than on mouthfuls
of fresh air, making a stir in the world
he'd just entered with something still a long way
from a roar, but all I could think of was
my mother's brother setting sail alone
on his voyage earlier that day,

his face a Belsen spectre of skin and bone,
his body invisible in the folds
of the bedclothes, and me listening to him
grinding out the last sound he'd ever make
in this world from the depths of his throat like stones
scraping the keel as Charon launched his boat.

Consider

Consider the unblinking perfection
of this utterly pitiless eye.
An eye being an eye to the heart of a stone.

Consider an eye that has never shed a tear
for being what it is and for what others are.
Consider a piece of matter ground out of a glacier.

Consider the eye of this falcon and the world as it is
and the eye of God flinching at the peephole of a star.

Surrender

In the blue distance a wisp of migrant
wild geese; sheep and sheep-droppings; daffodil clumps
in the close-cropped grass above the sea. I am

lying half-asleep on a bed of last year's
crackling bracken with Muckish at my back
and at my feet a rucked and pleated strand.

The sheep scatter: someone behind the hill
is attacking me with volleys of dry sheepdung.
I know it is you come to return me

to the holy ground of childhood, to clay
and roots and walking with God through incense
and flowers. I know you will not leave me

alone as over the hill you come running
towards me, laughing, still firing sporadic volleys.
I surrender to love by returning its fire.

The Biographer: The Life and the Work

His best friend told him that he'd picked his nose,
liked fresh well-buttered bread without a crust,
wore socks in bed when he made love to Mags
and loved to eat the crud between his toes.

A man obsessed with innocence and lust,
romantic passion for a rich old bags,
master of the lyric who thought in prose:
this was someone he knew the way God knows.

Or so he thought until, purely by chance,
the truth emerged: this man made his living
out of telling lies and all he'd learned
from Mags and from his letters and his books,
and what he'd told his wife and she'd told him,
was art and not the story of his life.

The Sea Wind

We were the grand-parents doing our best to keep
up with both of you that April-minted day

under a clouded sky tinted faintly blue.
But not as blue as what in the distance we thought

were glimpses of the sea until we discovered they were
pools of bluebells awash among the trees.

You ran, we followed and kept calling you back
as you set the forest cloisters echoing with your shouts.

And then a sea wind suddenly carried the sound
of your voices away among the flowers with us still

trying hard to keep up before it carried away ours.

The Sea

for Frank Galligan

I know him. And I know his fields
and the way his stony acres are always
the last to turn green in the spring:
he lives on the wrong side of the hill.
I know that shape in the furrows at twilight too:
once tall and straight as his own scarecrow
but bent now under the weight
of a wind that will never relent.
And he knows me and my strange ways:
watching out for birds, stooping
down to look at a wild flower,
sitting under a tree with a welter
of words swirling round in my head.
So there. We know each other. For years.
And always we stop to talk about crops
and weather across stone walls
or ditches or across the burn
that's wider and deeper than the sea
separating the man I know
from the man that knows me.

A Place

for Jocelyn Braddell

Not the sort of place where you'll find daffodils
being harried by the winds of March or tides
of bluebells swelling coppices in May,
not that sort of picturesque place at all,
but one of those places where you can be yourself,
can simply be at ease with what you are
by just being there and opening your eyes and breathing air;
a flat anonymous commonplace space
where nothing dramatic ever happens
except that the sunshine so often keeps
losing out to showers and there's not a beach
or a scenic mountain anywhere in sight;
a place to which the tourists never come
even in good weather because it's not
the sort of place tourists are ever
expected to go and where a bleached skull
is all that's left of a blackface ewe
that died there last summer beside the cracked rock
in the heather that's always wedged with shadow;
one of those places beyond all knowing and telling
with as much of a claim to being places
as Errigal, Glenveagh or Slieve League,
an empty desolate nameless space dense
with ordinariness and deity.

The Sheets

He did it in the dark: that handsome face,
a gargoyle to her now, grimacing above her.
Some nights it was hands: his paws on her;
hers suddenly paralysed; some nights teeth:
his on the nape of her neck; hers gnashing.
Daddy, she'd try, *Daddy, stop, stop, it's your Flossie!*
Her arms stretched out under him like a cross.

And morning would come with maybe the birds
singing or the shadows of trees dancing
on the ceiling and the Sacred Heart and sheets
her mother had made with her own hands that she'd
now have to wash and scrub until they were
as clean and white as her soul had once been.

Making Space

They came today and I made space for them
among all these letters, manuscripts and books
the way I used to make space here years ago
for their mothers because making space
is one of the things people who love
one another always do. And now it's
coming near the time for someone
to start thinking of making space somewhere for me.
Wherever that is I'm sure it will be
as private and as resonantly silent
as this place here has turned out to be.

But it's not something anyone here mentions
much to me, nor I to them, not even after
what happened some time ago and the doctor came.
A place I never gave much thought to
when their mothers were young.
Or when their children were here today and sang a song.
Only afterwards when they were gone.

The Sweeneyiad

Sweeney was full of it and long before
the Brits came and made Brit-bashing the name
of the game he was getting good mileage
out of Ireland's bloodymindedness:
the cold and wet, the stones and the thorns,
no place to lay his head, an enemy
behind every bush, tears as big as cloudbursts
coursing down his cheeks, fantasising
about women in the fork of a tree, going
on endlessly about his wretchedness
to a growing audience of starving fleas
he had to be careful not to incommode
in case they might decide to move house
and reduce his capacity for suffering more;
his head full of grievances and sodden lice
and romantic clap-trap about heritage sites
he had probably littered with kitchen
refuse and mounds of you-know-what;
yapping about beauty spots he'd seen
only once through poitin-tinted mists
and always the agony wasn't quite

agonising enough to satisfy
his superhuman capacity
for lamentation and pitying himself.

O Sweeney, Sweeney, how you loved the whining note—
Alas the day! Ochon! Woe is me!—
how you'd love to be around here now
doing your best to enrage the Celtic Tiger
by fuelling fires and boiling pots and trying
to ensure each of us should know who
he is against and what he is not
by wallowing in the wallow-holes
provided by the State to keep us from thinking
of the state we're in and convince Brussels
that a brand-new CAP should immediately begin!

Birdman, treeman, whinger, masochist, nut,
praiser of the past and everything that's not,
come down from your roost, *do* something for a change,
and we'll send you into Europe with a begging bowl
as dirty and capacious as the Irish Sea.
O Sweeney, Sweeney, you true-born Irishman,
give them ochons and the poor mouth as only you can!

News of the New World

Peace was too easy: how could this long-haired
one ever exchange his gun for a well-sprung
tart, grow fat-assed sitting in a chair,
die in bed; how could he ever close his heart
against their sad closed faces? In a land

impenetrable and dark as their minds,
far beyond the stridulant insects
and the fierce metallic rasping of the birds,
he heard the plotters in the static
of his dreams and when he woke at dawn he
saw a serpent's flickering specious tongue
withdraw behind their suddenly venomous eyes.

News of the Old World

At last peace came: the vultures, gorged, retired
from the feast but deep in the bush children
still died like flies. At once the victor, tired
but jubilant, accused a second foreign
power of infiltrating excess food
and issued orders for a numbered Swiss
bank account and fully automatic brand-
new bullet-proof Rolls Royce in gold for Miss

Eurasia and himself. And all went well
 until a bomb exploded in his Hall
of Heavenly Fame. They swept his jackals
from the corridors of power, the children
died once more, and when they led him from his cell
the vultures stirred: they smelt a dying lion.

Mountains

Ben Bulben's rucks and pleats, my own Slieve League
shimmering in seamist across the bay:
I saw them through a haze of grief that day
as we drove at speed through Sligo into Mayo
but found we were too late when we arrived.
The nuns had laid her out in cottons and linens
that matched the pallor of her hands and face.
I kissed her cheek and burned my lips on ice
and shed my tears and touched the lidded eyes.
Whatever final image of the world was locked
in there was locked in there forever now.
It was not one of me. Through the window
I could see Nephin sailing out of a cloud.
Not an image she'd ever have wanted to see
after listening so often to me going
on about going up mountains when she'd
always hated the bleakness of high ground
yet found herself there alone in the end.
And higher than I'd ever been. And needing
love's oxygen to help her to breathe
in that thin mountain air. And none there.
And mist coming down fast everywhere.

Bogspeak

For centuries I have been quaking
under the weight of well-shod feet.
None of them was capable of learning

that whoever walks on me walks on water.
If they put a foot wrong they drowned
in what only the wood-kerne knew was
bottomless solid ground.
In my fluid and devious
conspiracies with land and water
I have swallowed stepping stones
the way I have swallowed dolmens and crosses.
I thrive on the liquid diet
martyrdom has prescribed
for the saint and the hunger striker
and, carnivorous too like my daughter
the sundew, I sometimes regurgitate
the corpse of some informer I reluctantly ate.
Now and then the mist lifts to reveal
the substance of my fantasies dissolving
in sunlight but only for a moment
and soon I am fantasising again.
Enter me gently and never forget
what my loneliness masks: all my dreams are wet
and I keep coming under the pressure
of alien bodies I love to hate.

Sometimes with the sun's help I crack a dry joke.
Mostly I've been going up in puffs of smoke.
Bog-man, bog-bishop, bog-job:
I have a bad name: as many
as there are different kinds of wet weather
in the taxonomy of rain.
I flow slow and run deep: the lie of the land.
In summer you can hear me ticking
over like a clucking hen sitting
on the clutch of bombs
history lays and hatred slowly hatches.

Swans

come in at the ends of their tethers
lamenting like the Children of Lir
at their fate before they drown

their sorrows in the waters of the lake;
then have the neck to try and show us
that what we thought was a ramrod in flight

a few moments ago is really an s-bend
pipe that unbends and plumbs itself
to the bottom when they alight;

take to the land and shatter all the dreams
we ever had of ballerinas and *Swan Lake*;
watch the off-white waterfall

turn green with envy in the sea
but know it will have its revenge
when their cygnets first see the light of day;

are reputed to find their *real* voices
not long before the end and sing
the songs they're always dying to sing.

Estrangement

Grass still bent under the weight
of yesterday's rain;
black turds

of slugs; the white flash of birds
far out at sea
like flurries

of purposeful snow and you,
withdrawn and inviolable
this morning

as the mountain in its habit
of mist, your eyes opaque
with distance,

the sea on my lips salt
as last night's
tide of tears.

Watching How It Happens

Under creased tea-stained tissue-paper skin
the veins on the backs of his hands

surface like the gnarled roots of old trees.
When he rises from a chair or climbs the stairs

he creaks and whistles like the timbers
and rigging of a ship in a storm at sea.

The child that he was is the ghost beginning
to haunt the ruins he thinks is a man.

I watch the old growing old by watching myself.

Birches

Birches in leaf are girls
in their summer dresses.
Even in winter they remain
different: they strip
better and their skin
gleams after rain.
They stand naked
and unashamed, frail
as porcelain, and utterly
feminine.

Foxgloves

for Matthew Sweeney

went topless long before it was
fashionable and let all hang

out shamelessly over grass banks
and low stone walls like harlots leaning

over their half-doors. They're plastered
with rouge and weighed down with as many

love-bitten breasts as the statue
of a crumbling eastern goddess—

and look how each one of them's mottled
with beauty spots like a trout!

But it's all up front, there's nothing behind:
when they're past it and poxed

and wasting away you can see
they were mostly vertebrae.

A Poem For Kieran

that he may always find wonder
in a clutch of eggs in a wildbird's nest
or the print the hare left last night in the long grass
and dream of some day finding a mermaid's
love letter in a beached bottle
with kisses like starfish shining on every page.

133

Love and Peace

My daughter painted the words
LOVE and PEACE on our crumbless
bird-table. I suspect that birds are
illiterate and in favour
of brash aggression; certainly,
being sometimes near starvation,
they'd hardly relish the irony
in this moral exhortation.

Crumbs, not words, are strictly for the birds.

Dryad

The sounds and smells of felling. And then we came
on the fellers and on the toppled
trunks and scattered limbs of all these trees
that not long ago had cradled birds
and clutched at the skirts of clouds
but now lay like slaughtered innocents
on a battlefield. It was the fate of one
that moved us most: a birch tall and slender
as our eldest daughter and the only
birch among these groves of conifers.
Its peeling bark was the exact shade
of a horse chestnut before the light
darkens it and yellows the white velvet
mould into which it was poured.
At the merest touch of the saw's teeth it

toppled to the ground and something
that was neither a leaf nor a leaf's shadow nor a bird
fluttered out of its foliage and disappeared.
What was that, you asked, was it a bird?
But I had nothing to say, not a word.

Epistemology

She is singing to herself in the kitchen.
A song about youth and love. Age has not
yet sucked all the sweetness out of a voice

that reaches me faintly as I lie in bed
reading in the room above. I listen.
A new note has crept into her voice

and suddenly a stranger is singing the song
in a way I'd never heard her sing it before.
All those years of sharing, of secrets uncovered,

laughter, tears, all those mysteries love
unlocks from the heart kiss by kiss, I knew *her*
but *who* was this? An ageing woman is

singing to herself in the kitchen below while
an ageing man in bed upstairs is reading
Bertrand Russell on how we know what we know.

A Classicist in the Blue Stacks

The day that I went up to Meenaguise
and helped to draw some water from Bob's well

and Bob began to talk of Plato's Greek
that would have been all Greek to me I knew

I'd come as close as I would ever come
to something like a source because when you

go drawing water from Bob Bernen's well
you're drawing more than water from a well.

Dowsing

for Caitríona McNamara

There is something going on here today
that was not going on here yesterday,

the stir of some subterranean force
as, the pen in my hand poised over the paper

like a hazel rod in the hands of a dowser,
I am suddenly brimming over

with the mystery of words that lie
far deeper underground than water

yet come spurting up until I plug
their flow with this full stop.

St. Columb's

In memoriam Derek Hill

A house as full of subtle light and shade
as one of the pictures hanging on its walls
smoulders like a Monet poppy among trees
and the shadows of trees. The blue
of the hall is the blue of a god's eye
and the lake borrows and ruffles the blue
of the sky. Two horse-chestnuts gravely
acknowledge the breeze and I acknowledge
the Berensonian eye for beauty
that has been at work here as sedulously
as these bees at work among the peonies.
And suddenly I have a sense of someone
from Parnassus waiting in the wings
to announce a dance of nymphs and fauns
around the slender white columns growing on the lawn.

A Poem For Garbhan

that he may one day find enlightenment
in deciphering the symbols gulls print
on the beach with their feet and love
in the sweet nothings larks make into songs
to storm heaven with all day long.

In Memory Of Lawson Burch 1937-1999

Ardara, Glenties, Rosbeg, Narin, Portnoo:
those were your favourite stamping grounds.
You knew where you stood when you stood there.
And whether you were one of the throng in Nancy's,
a glass in your hand, that glint in your eye
maybe hinting at some new story on the way,
or paying your tributes in painterly skill
to the Master himself of your art and mine
by making your own world lit with your own light
on canvases as bare and white as the void could have been,
I knew you were always drawn to the high ground.
And that's what you always found around here
and suddenly walked right through the arch
of a rainbow still wet with a paint
you'd had your eye on for years in the glens
and never wanted to walk back out again.
I can guess what you said to the Master up there.
What sort of a brush do you think I should use on thin air?

New Poems

Beachcombings

SCULPTORS

In memory of Con O'Mullane

It sits on my desk being nothing but what
I know it to be: a perfection of form.
The stone that we found washed up on the shore
at Enniscrone more than fifty years ago.
Smooth as flesh stretched over bone and shaped
so sensuously by the sea I can't keep
my hands off it each time it catches my eye.
Like that Brancusi we saw in London once
and kept on wanting to touch and touch and touch.

LOOKING DOWN AT THE SKY

Look at that mad stargazer studying
astronomy by looking at the sand
where the receding tide's left a single
starfish and added a tail to each one
of the countless tiny shells embedded
like comets in the sky on the strand.

A BRIEF HISTORY OF TIME

That time I followed the arrows a bird
had inscribed on the sand with its feet
was the time I realised the arrow
of time was the time I wasted following
what was pointing me forward by leading me back.

ALTER EGO

The day you told me I had two faces
was the day I was walking on wet sand
towards Moyne Hill and, with each step I took,
watched another step ghosting and unghosting
on the strand around the prints of my feet.

HAREBELLS

On a sunny day of late summer
a flight of estuary waders
preparing for touchdown
warily circles the machair
confused by a quivering array
of blue windsocks indicating
a steady force six blowing
from every conceivable point of the compass.

MIRROR MIRROR ON THE STRAND

Here I am again space-walking
through the sky and the clouds looking
at myself looking for words
to describe what the tide
has provided for the vanity
of me and a flock of preening birds.

Lugworm

If I could join together these pieces
of string heaped on the beach I'd have a line
long enough to fly a kite to heaven
or plumb the ocean's deepest abysses.

The Mathematicians

God, you said, with a sweep of your hand
taking in the big picture
of sky and sea, had to be
a mathematician but I
was looking at the small picture
as the marram grass bent to its task
of drawing circles and half circles
on the sand as perfect as the ones
I used to draw at school with compasses.

Fruits of the Sea

Look how today on a distant sandbank
in the estuary where clouds are shoaling
the seals are curled up like black bananas.

Barnacles

I've found a vast mountain landscape
of extinct volcanoes,
each one the shape of a cone,
on this tiny seashore stone.

SANDHOPPERS

A cloudless blue sky and the patter
of raindrops that, no matter
how long they fall, will never wet a single one
of these windrows of seaweed drying in the sun.

THE CRYPTOGRAPHERS

When it's not drawing circles and half circles,
what the marram grass inscribes on the sand
with the fine point of its rusting nib is
as enigmatic as the cryptograms
these flocks of waders have printed with their feet.

CHINOISERIE

The eyes of the girl with the pigtail
in the coolie hat on an Irish beach
among the tiny pagodas of sea sandwort
go suddenly Chinese in the sun's glare
as she places the willow-patterned dish
of picnic sandwiches
on the reed mat made in Hong Kong.

THE TIRELESS SEAMSTRESS

The incoming tide that unstitches
the seams and irons out
the tucks and pleats
in this beach's cloth-of-gold
will shortly recede and leave

new seams, tucks and pleats, holes
in the cloth-of-gold
for the next incoming tide
to unstitch, iron out, darn,
on and on *ad infinitum*.

WALKIES AND TALKIES

The ringed plover, dashing about the beach
in spurts of manic energy,
seems intent on showing me
and the dog how frantically
it's been rehearsing for its role
in the next early Chaplin movie
until the dog decides to become
a barker for the talkies
and the plover goes walkies
in a way that would not be possible
for Chaplin or the dog or me.

BLUEBELLS

June and, as I was caught out
telling a lie to you,
a shimmer of blue and green
on a grassy islet
in Loughros Beg Bay
was striving unsuccessfully
to counterfeit aquamarine.

DUNLIN

Far out over the sea
in a sunlit sky
feathered with white cloudlets
constellations of stars
twinkle in broad daylight.

THE SUNBATHERS

Although she is voluptuously beautiful
and he seems besotted with his Janet
(I lost count of all the times he uttered her name)

I think that she may have a heart of stone
because I saw the sweat beads glisten
in the pores of her flesh like mica in granite.

LICHEN

I would never have imagined
that the pavement beside the beach
at Portnoo would be white
with discs of chewing gum
until I suddenly realised
that nature can be a litter-lout too.

KNOTS

A puff of smoke whipped away
from a chimney but I know
it's not from Patrick's house

on the headland when it
suddenly changes direction
and veers into the wind
without reducing speed.

THE NEGATIVE

The sea has receded
to the horizon
but the rippling wavelets
I am paddling through dry-shod
is the negative
of a still photograph
it took of itself on the strand.

TARGET

The brent geese appear and disappear
in the rise and fall of the swell. So, now that
Moohan's Amusements are back
in town, come to the rifle-range
side-show and take aim.

REHEARSAL

Hand in hand
on the beach
in the misty distance
I watch the lovers
in their *pas de deux*
two into one
and one into two.

THE SEA GIRAFFES

When I took ages today
on the beach
to immerse myself
in the sunlit sea
I could hear your laughs
as I swathed myself
in the rippling pelts
of herds of giraffes.

THE SKY WRITERS

Out over the sea on the slate-blue sky
flocks of small waders try to translate the symbols
they wrote on the beach with their feet
but they're wasting their time
if they think doodles like that
will fool even an ignoramus like me.

ONE

A grey day at Murvagh
and the sea and the sky
so inseparably seamlessly one
it seems they will never be
parted again
by the horizon.

SNOW IN SUMMER

That August day when I found
a gannet
the tide had washed up
on the shore dead
I thought of the first time
I'd pissed in snow
as I looked
at its neck and head.

MUSSELS

When I saw them in the distance I said
why would Donegal County Council want
to tarmacadam the rocks on Dooey Strand.

THE SKYLARK

was a singing speck in the sky
far above their heads
as the lambs in the dunes below
were showing it how even the earth-bound
are able to go skylarking on the ground.

Epiphany in Ardnamona

Looking up through the leaves
of a birch at the blue
of the sky I am taken
out of the shadow of myself
through the light in my eye.

The Snow Moths

The only reason I am picking
these snowberries
hanging in a hedgerow near here
is because I have seen the holes
that were eaten in a blanket of snow
lying under this dripping sycamore tree.

No Hands

The sound of no hands
clapping is a pigeon
in the glen applauding
a dog and two sheepmen
herding a huge flock of ewes
into a tiny pen.

No Boards

The sound of no boards
creaking is the sound
of a tree rehearsing
its reincarnation
in the timbers
of a boat at sea.

Reflection

Is that great tit now fiercely attacking
itself in the glass of my window pane
trying to tell me that what it doesn't know
is no reason for me not to know
that I am my own worst enemy.

Slieve League

My astonishment that winter's day
in summer was to climb
and find two windswept orchids
purple with cold sheltering
behind some summit stones
like the two girls in summer frocks
I once found shivering
behind a rock on Blue Stack.

The Difference

Tory again this summer after long absence
and thirty-four corncrakes we were too late to hear
and having to look up a book to confirm
what we saw for the first time ever
with our own two eyes under a clouded sun:
a golden eagle that Balor
would have known instantly with his one.

Tulip

Two dogs barking beside lakewater.
The swan glides away from them:
a flurry of ruffled petals
and a stiff misplaced stem.

Living Art

Look at it. In sunshine
threaded with rain
a great tit
hangs upside down
from our brand-new feeder:
white, yellow banded with black,
a convex living abstract
botched by Mondrian.

Choughs

live rough on the wilder shores
of this distant littoral.
Such elegant high-fliers
cutting a dash
over machair and cairn
plastered with lipstick
and dressed to impress
in their black plastic macs
and thigh-high red boots
but wasting their fine feathers
on our John Paddy Dan
who just lumps them with crows
and crows, he says, should be shot at sight.

Heliography

The blades of the oars
of the fisherman's boat
creasing the blue silk
of Lough Eske flash silver
in the sinking sun to answer
the flash of a windscreen
turning gold in Lacrum.
Is it asking him how he's done?

Wild Life on One

Such amorous passion in the long grass,
such an overpowering embrace!
I can imagine the endearments
he might whisper in her ear.
I love you so much I could eat you.
And he will, he will,
never so close to the other
as when we make love or kill.

Transference

What I noticed when I took you with me
to dip your right hand in the holy well
was the number of warts that were growing
on the bark of each of the bourtrees there.

Wintering

They've grown old as we've grown old and now
flaunt masses of ringlets as white
as the doilies of snow spread out at their feet.
I said they were like wizened old women trying
to be young girls, grotesque, but you said
if I'd wintered as well as these willowherbs
in a field near Lough Eske I'd have more to flaunt
than my misogyny and my bald head.

Eating the Scenery

Farmers say you can't eat the scenery
but in Dunlewey you can because there's
a church there that, as well as being part
of the beauty of the place, looks good enough to eat.
A marzipan confection that might have fallen
from a deliciously baroque wedding cake.
If the cows and the sheep there had a sweet tooth
they'd have nibbled it away long before now.
I love it so much myself I could devour it.
And I would except for the fact that
the Poisoned Glen's just a stone's throw away.
Too close for comfort. And anyway,
to be on the safe side, I only go there
in Lent when I'm off the sweets.

Occasion of Sin

A cloud suddenly sweeps up a nail-clipping of moon.
She's astir in the dark like the sea in the sound.
She tempts me closer with a moaning sigh and now
the warm smell of her ebbs and flows through the June night.
I am taking pleasure in the heavy breathing
of Manus O'Doherty's recently bulled cow.

Appearance and Reality

When someone remarks you look like me why do
I fail to find a feature of my face
in yours? What can I say to them except

what's true? Presence enough my absence here
in you has been to me. I look deeper
than the you I see under appearance

to reality. What's me in you may
not be what I see but you are
my daughter because you came out of me.

Two Realists and a Romantic on Slieve League

We have reached the summit again. Last time
we did it together we climbed in the rain
but today the weather is better

and a mist from the sea swirls over the stream
and a furious stonechat scolding us
from the scree. A delicate red sandal

lies abandoned by the track and, incurably
romantic, I wonder whether the girl
who wore it was pretty or plain,

blonde or black, but you said she was probably
old and fat and if she climbed mountains
in sandals like that deserved what you hoped

she'd got: a damn good scolding from an outraged stonechat.

Work Ethic

Not knowing much of hedges or hedging,
having lived for long in a land of stone

walls and done mostly walling, I've only just
noticed how often hedging down here seems

a matter of simply doing nothing at all,
unlike walling which no one can do

by default but only stone by stone.

The Last of the Snow

What are those patches of white I see
through a gap in the trees? They remind

me of something I used to see long ago
in the fields but when I come closer

I see it's the last of the snow and will go
the same way as my mother and the sheets

she used to spread out on the grass to bleach.

Malinbeg

Choughs strut and chatter among the whins;
a cloud fits itself to the mountain;
the seawind's warm as breath on my face;

water shapes and shines itself on stone;
the sun is a white disc and I am thinking
of that luminous summer of the flesh

years ago when, first light filtering through
the curtains, the lineaments of a sleeping face
would take shape on the pillow beside me

the way now the ghost of the sun that was
haunting a cloud has slowly begun
to materialise and blind me.

Getting Through

> "Truth is subjectivity"— Kierkegaard

Pascal and the rationalising heart,
Hume undermining reason with reason,
and Kierkegaard, another gloomy Dane,
showing us how to muster up enough
passion to contemplate making a call
to that ex-directory number whose
discovery depends on nothing so
much as on how you despair of ever

making contact with someone you'll only
get through to when he's simultaneously
trying to get through to you on a line jammed
with intertwined fibres of heart and mind.
Listen. The God of the philosophers
is philosophical. *I am what I am.*

Salt

Sin? Now, tell me about that.
How does the soul retain
its buoyancy with such a freight?
To live is to live in a house
of matter but souls ride the waves
of a sea replenished by rivers
whose source is a mystery.
So salt that sea but not always
salt enough to keep afloat
the small boat of one's soul
and its shifting cargo of sin.
And what of man in his house of matter?
Man is the salt of the earth.
And the sea? The sea is
the salt of his tears.
And sin? Sin is a measure
of the salt God failed to add in.

Symmetry

Once, when she'd undressed and was getting
me ready for bed, she saw me looking
at the contours I'd never seen uncovered.
A laugh and the white flash of her nightgown
and I saw two mounds of jelly topped with cherries.
Years later, when I had a gooseberry chin,
I used to watch her making apple jelly
by filling a white cloth with apple mush
and hanging it from a rafter in the ceiling.
I'd stand in the back pantry looking up
at the great pendulous breast with its translucent
amber nipple forming and reforming
as it slowly dripped into a bucket.
But somewhere deep inside me was another
yearning. What it wanted was symmetry.

The Potato House

It was one of those outhouses with no windows
and a clay floor. I liked that and I liked
even more to stand there in the darkness
behind the closed door and share my ferment
with the ferment of a small mountain
of seed potatoes that were all eyes for
the gleeds of light leaking in through the keyhole
and the slit at the bottom of the door.

When I drew breath there it was like being
a root in the earth yearning for light,
it was the reek of seed and sickly white
shoots like squeezed blackheads and it was where
I first learned how the hairs I was sprouting
would darken more than my chin and my crotch.

Medals and Mayflowers

It was the time when, going to confession
or benediction, we'd avoid the man
with the evil eye by crossing the street
to the other side, the time when, on our way
to early Mass, we'd step over the mayflowers
scattered around our doors and windows
to keep the fairies at bay, but most of all

it was the night when I, a baptised child
of Christ with a holy medal on a chain
around my neck, was lifted up in her arms
in the garden clutching a silver coin
to show to the new moon that was floating
in a cloudless sky like a wood-shaving
fallen from St. Joseph's work-bench in Heaven.

The Furies

I signed a form to give away the heart
I'd pledged to you and gave them access
to that lump of butchers' meat that houses
love and hate, joy, rage, and fear. They sawed through
flesh and bone into my chest and stopped my heart
and mended it and started it again.
If stopping hearts is death then I *was* dead
except that I was hooked to a machine

and ceased to hear old voices whispering
new terrors in my ear. I died to live,
to smell a rose or walk the glen, to gather
love around me like a cloak hiding me
from them. But when I rose from death they shrieked:
Old man, you died to live to die again!

Convalescence

Here I am back in my own place again
looking at the mountain emerge dripping
wet from the womb of a cloud that's
already preparing its shroud;
noting how the bole of the dead alder
outside this window is feathered with ivy
like the legs of a bird of prey; here I am
again observing the Zeitgeist
gnawing its way into the marrow
of an old language like a dog with a soul

163

and seepage from the loins of those
two old whoremasters, war and politics,
still tainting the waters of the purest wells;
here I am ensconced in therapies
like a Rosses cow knee-deep in Meath grass
with my ear to the ground listening
to the thunder of worms turning
in the clay growing fainter every day.

Consulting the Oracle at Inis Ceithleann

Unless you're born on the island you're
not considered to be a true native here.
So who am I then and what's my fate
if I'm neither an insular Celt
nor a mainland Planter? A bog-trotter
with a foot in both camps and the folly
of thinking that I won't lose more than face
if I'm tempted to turn the other cheek?

Listen to me and know that you are doomed
to cross and recross the embattled
bridgeheads of yourself and feel, mingling
within you, the eddies and currents
of streams love once united in the veins
of the living: the blood of the dead.

Selves

It is going down the mountain
again after going up
past the high lakes

most never see
that aches in the heart
like love lost.

I climb all year unless
there is snow and you
go with me

but, mostly I do it alone.
It is best days the sun
picks out small streams

silver as snail tracks,
cataracts so far off they are
chalk marks

on the dark slopes, and stones
so wholly lost to themselves
they are like

the souls of saints as I sit down
in the sun or rain trying
to empty myself

of myself and learn
the art of silence
from a cloud.

Then

That time will come. We won't have long to wait.
And if it's me, and you might sometimes think
of looking for what's gone by looking here,
look elsewhere. And forget those photographs.
Whoever's there, you'll know it is not me.
My ring, a snippet of my hair? I know
you well enough to know you'll never be
a sentimentalist like me. So what?
Take heart—what else? —and go and find someone
whose love you know was always strong and true.
Just hold her in your arms as I held you
and look into her eyes and know what's left
of me on earth is looking back at you.
And know that she's your daughter. And mine too.

Cosmologies

We'd always been Copernicans but she
still clung to Ptolemy's cosmology
as both of us scanned eyes now full of signs
and wonders we'd not seen before. We were
a pair of stargazers and what we saw
emerging into view was the dark side
of a satellite that imagined it was
reversing a cosmological law.

So there she was in orbit round this heavenly body
she thought was in orbit round her and here
we were expounding love's cosmology
to what was a deaf ear: how satellites
glorying in reflected light are bound
by the laws of heliocentricity.

Luna

for Clare McDonnell

Little white moonfaces,
squat fat Buddhas,
totems

constellating the firmament
of darkening grass;
the night so still it seems

to hold its breath.
I smell honeysuckle
and the sea as I kneel

to decapitate them
one by one between fingers
and thumb. The moon is out,

barbarous among the stars,
demanding adoration,
and soon I am prostrate

among the plundered constellations,
inhaling essences,
the smell of death so pure

and fresh it could be
the death of angels
or of innocence.

The Botany of Love

The five-fingered palmate
leaf of the sycamore
on which these ladybirds mate
has a stem that's as red
as your flushed cheeks are now
when you suddenly discover
that although I am complaisant
and your lover you have not
got *me* in the palm of your hand.

Longevity

I've spent half a day sitting here trying
to write a poem that might live as long
as the castle in Donegal Town
or even as long as this Lough Eske
drystone wall that's beginning to crumble
and disintegrate like the poet now
grateful it's still strong enough to bear his weight.

The Wrong Note

I knew when I'd said it that I'd rubbed you the wrong way.
You ceased talking and flounced off past an oak
where a robin was singing wistfully.

I stopped to listen and whistled back
but the robin stayed silent, then flew away,
and I knew I'd struck the wrong note twice in the same day.

Anne

I never gave much thought to you for years.
You never figured in my dreams or tears.

What was the colour of your hair and eyes?
Who's left to tell me what's the truth or lies?

The past's a phantom glimpsed through winter mists.
Could I have really watched two tiny fists

once crumple and uncrumple like a fern?
Is yours that unmarked grave beside the Erne?

Were you laid out like adults on a bed,
was your coffin white, had I tears to shed?

I need something to anchor me to you—
a single hair, a photograph might do—

something to sweeten what has been the fate
of one who's loved too little and too late

but what have I except I know you're dead
and once a priest poured water on your head?

Dear infant sister, Anne, I stake my claim
to love you now on all I know. Your name.

The Hawthorn and the Cherry

after A.E. Housman

Loveliest of trees, the hawthorn now
is hung with bloom along the bough,
and stands about the mountainside
wearing white for Whitsuntide.

Now, if I reach fourscore and ten
eighty years won't come again
and take from ninety springs fourscore
at best it leaves me ten springs more,

and since I have such little time
and braes are harder now to climb
about the hillsides I will go
to see the hawthorn hung with snow

until, Housman, like Jack the Glen,
I reach my fourscore years and ten
and then to Shropshire I will go
to see the cherry hung with snow.

The Singer

A bagful of blood and guts
hung on a tree of bone
more akin to the cloddish earth
than a spirit shaped by a god;
yet this clod rises and sings.
Even Pegasus had wings.

The Preacher

He looked leonine with that mane of hair
and, what was more, he *was* leonine when
he smiled to bare his teeth and prepared to roar.
They flocked to hear him, didn't think it odd
that he should keep preaching the word of God
more like a lion than one of God's sheep.
Sin was what Eve whispered in Adam's ear,
he thundered nightly. Who could fail to hear?

His children loved him: bear hugs and kisses
were the order of the day and long hours
silently watching them play. What they couldn't
understand when allowed to watch TV
was how the lion they saw there could be
the lamb they frisked about with after tea.

A Dream of Numbers

A, e, i, o, u. We knew from the beginning
how we'd never be able to resist
you and your mellifluous enticements.
At first it was chaste monosyllabic kisses
but when we finally lost our virginity
in the promiscuity of the polysyllabic
the word was born in pristine splendour.
In no time at all we were indulging
in sesquipedalian orgies.
The dewfalls of genesis jewelled us
but some of us began to lose our radiance
the moment men spoke us or wrote us down.
Time smeared us with a thin scum of usage.
Purity was a dream of prelapsarian
consonants lean and hard as desert fathers.
Our progeny began to fill the shelves
of the bookshops and libraries of the world.
We became the toys of hermetic masters
and the aphrodisiacs of lurid pornographers.
Borges came and lived among us like a metaphor,
strengthened our belief in the ontology
of the verbal, we embodied ourselves in Joyce who
imagined he was writing what was us writing him.
Prophets and mystics enlisted us
to describe the indescribable.

What hubris! The angels wept for us.
Wittgenstein confirmed our limitations:
Whereof one cannot speak, thereon one must be silent.
Beckett took us on the long journey
towards the silence encoded in nature by God
but we knew that what lay beyond us
was there before us and would be there after us.
We sank beneath the weight of centuries
of dross and, yearning for a new identity,
began to look with envy on the toys
the new masters played with now: austere
tautologies, theorems, axioms, equations
unsmeared with what contaminated us.
It was only then that we began
to dream of one day becoming numbers.

An Old Man Looks at a Storm-Twisted Beech

What you are doing this winter's day
is beyond me. I am an old man
and have to keep my feet firmly
on the ground. You are feminine
and aspire in midair to sensuous
and voluptuous ways not mine. I am
singular, you are plural
and, apparently, lesbian: all curves,
orifices, waists, hips, beauty spots,
fat blubbery lips for wet kisses,
mouths that pout and pucker
or, tongued with fern, open wide
in a rictus of unimaginable sensuality.

I can see blue sky in the eye
of the needle between your thighs
above the matt black lichen of your
stocking tops. Boldly you offer your
breasts for love -as many as the foxglove
does but firmer and less pendulous.
In places your limbs are locked in such
convolute embraces you look as if
you have been reading the Kama Sutra.
Sometimes you come under the heat
of an intermittent sun and steam: vulva, buttocks.
What would once have turned me on is the texture
of your bark under the palms of my hands:
smooth, taut, sensuous: a young girl's skin
even an old man like me can take some pleasure in.

The Death of Romance

She imagined it would be the breath
of the breeze on the grass of a meadow,
a girl dancing with her own shadow,
the sweetness of a bee rifling nectar from a flower,
until he showed her it was a tree
groaning and threshing about
in the arms of a storm,
a reek of the sea's abysses,
tooth-and-nail caresses,
predatory kisses.

St. Kilda 1903

He brought it back after his first visit
to the mainland but showed it to no one.
Not even to her. She saw him staring
at it many times when he thought that there
was no one looking. Until one day she
searched through his pockets when he was asleep
and found it wrapped in a piece of sailcloth.
She unwrapped it, stared at it with wonder
for a long time. There was nothing like it
anywhere on the island. Then she said
to herself: *She's nothing much to look at.*
And put the mirror back in his pocket.

The Old Poet

has always known how to make an art out
of dereliction and now waits patiently
for the muse like a scarecrow
waiting to be animated by the wind.
Keratoses begin to grow out of his head.
His enemies call them horns.
He tries to retain a child's sense of wonder
without descending into childishness
and hates his muse for being so generous
with her favours to the young and beautiful.
He keeps losing things: poems, old friends,
his hair, sometimes even the run of himself.
Everything except his abrasive tongue

and the yellowing teeth he bares
to bite the hand that feeds him
or pretend he's smiling when his muse attempts
to ingratiate herself with him once more.
Poems are oases in the encroaching desert
of old age. Sometimes mirages.
He tries hard not to call his muse a whore.

Gannet

Marauder. One of a raiding party
from The Stags or Ailsa Craig maybe.
Mission today the soft target of Donegal Bay.
A painted aboriginal face
or something missing from the natural history
museum's collection of tribal masks.
El Greco at work in stained glass.
The bow that is its own arrow.
Whiter than the white the sea bleeds where he
furls himself in the water like an umbrella
pretending it's not raining in wet weather.

Narcissus

Nights and he dreamed of nothing but the dawn.
Day after day he saw curious faces
peer at him through the leaves of the willows
but she was the most beautiful of all,
the shimmering porcelain of her face
shining in the pools of that haunted place
until, demented, he plunged in, all hot
and thrashing passion, and entered the cave
of self-delight between the two white cascades
that were the pillars of her thighs and, locked
in the fierceness of his own embrace,
seed spilling in the river dims like milt,
found what he had always been afraid to find.
And afterwards loved no one but himself.

Dylan Thomas in Glenlough

A grief ago beside the ruck-and-pluck of the sea
he shouted wonders to the summer hills.
Only the sheep the birds listened
to the echoes
dying dying
happy as the grass is green
a boy singing singing.
O listen now the echoes still go
ringing ringing:
I see a boy of summer in his ruin -ruin -ruin!

177

Nancy's

for Margaret

What more can you really expect from a pub
but good drink, convivial company and,
when the time comes, to be able to go out
and empty your bladder against a wall where,
swaying on the see-saw of a loose flag
in the floor and inhaling the odours
of all the roses crowding in through
the open window of the W.C. brings
a sort of drunkenness even to sobriety.

The Fly

The roomful of eyes, having nowhere to look now
but into more eyes, follows the flight of a fly
in erratic orbit around the light bulb.
A chorus of neighbourhood crones stage-whispers
its comments as each new arrival crosses the floor
and an old island man with rheum in his eyes
creaks over loose boards into a chair.
The hair of the daughter who married too late
is white at the roots and Cathal from Glen
is saying how much someone I never saw
in my life before and no one else here
has ever seen darken their doors looks like himself.

Looks like himself? That man there
who can't even raise a hand to brush off
the fly that's now settled on one white lidded eye
like the first sign of flesh reverting to clay?
The only way he'd ever look like himself
would be if he took a breath of fresh air.

Springcleaning

He left her clearing out an old wardrobe
they'd not used for years and walked
out into the springclean light.
Into a skein of wild geese
on a loose leash over Blue Stack,
the flicker of wheatears
through wisps of iridescent mist,
the unfleeced sun drying a patina
of green from the skull of a dead ewe
and a scummed stone and, when he came back,
into her holding a crumpled blue dress
in her hands. It smelt of mothballs.
She said it was the one she'd worn away
on their wedding day and she'd just
found it by chance in the old wardrobe upstairs.
He vaguely remembered the dress but how could
he forget what she was wearing that night
years ago when it fell to the floor.
The one that needed mothballs.
Not the one he liked so much more.

The Kiss

He was never one for showing emotion
in a public place or even holding hands
when they were walking out together
but he was a different creature
when no one else was there
and so it was that when the time came
to fasten down the coffin lid
she thought it only right to ask
for a few moments alone with him
and closed the door and had one
long last look and bent down
and kissed the ice-cold lips
that would never be kissed again.
She knew he would have liked that
because no one else was there.
No one, she thought, not even himself.

The Archway

How beautiful the archway framing
a single tree
and a view of the distant hills.
How beautiful the archway
that might have turned into a cave
but certainly never a womb:
the wind is too cold in the archway,
the light too strong.

I stand in the archway and dream
of a womb framing a view
of a single tree
and the distant hills.

Partings

Such jealousies as once their partings bred
in him—the air she breathed and he did not;
her imprint on another's heart perhaps;
strangers who dared to look her in the eye;
her secret places and his absence there—
such jealousies were roots that never flowered.
Desire deranged him then: he took and she
gave him what he couldn't give to her until
that final parting came and love came too
and nailed him to a cross he wished that he
could coffin with her body in the grave.

A Tanka and Four Haiku

Your cold white hands that
cage this huge crucifix once
caged me with love but
why does that bird outside beat
against the corpse-room window?

Why am I afraid
to open this silver box
full of a child's hair?

Why do you sigh in
your sleep? Why does the night wind
sigh in the aspen?

The dove hides in the
oak's shadow but who will hide
in the hawk's shadow?

The sapling quivers
after the bird has flown and
the hawk's craw is full.

Mindset

He's walking on a woodland track
at twilight along the Border
and hooks his foot in a bramble
that's strayed across the path. He knows
he's safe in the instant his mind
has time to register tripwire.

Dandelion

Starved of colour after the long winter
and enjoying the warm March sunshine,
we welcome that first bright blaze
of yellow we might even concede
to be a flower but which, later on,
when it's joined by throngs of others
on the lawn and its coiffure's
Afro-white, we'll call a weed.

Value

I could talk for hours about mountains, lakes,
flowers, or how the light in the sky
at sunset sometimes radiates like the spokes
of a wheel from the hub of a cloud, things

like that, but I wouldn't, not because you'd
be bored having to listen, which some
of you would, but because you'd be getting
for nothing something that others who *read* what
I've written have probably paid for
in cash and, as a result, will value far more.

Commercial

Even in this guttering light
Barnesmore's something to write home about:
the last few shreds of shrinking snow
a tinker's washing of off-white scraps;
Blue Stack makes a more bourgeois impact
with a neat snowline of wind-bleached sheets
but the Grey Mare's Tail's worked up the finest lather
of all: nothing washes whiter than a waterfall.

Disabilities

James has put up notices on the bit
of scrub he owns warning trespassers off
and now a pair of home-building stonechats
has taken possession of the same land
and are always there haranguing people
as they pass on their way to the shop.
So now James has become a trespasser
on his own land, the stonechats trespassers
on land they are certain belongs to them.

But you'd be wrong if you thought this could lead
to violence, an appearance in court.
James is stone-deaf and if you're reading this
you're doing something the stonechats can't do.

Kinship

The old fencing posts,
bearded with lichen,
bent, emaciate,
struggle up
the mountainside
in single file
but suddenly stop
at the tree-line
as if fearful of leaving
their kith and kin behind.

Evidence

I knew the storm that thrashed
the grove last night
was severe
when I saw the blisters
it raised on the bole
of this conifer here.

Copycat

The jet forging the links of a white chain
in the blue sky is trying to copy
the chains streams have forged on the mountain-side
after last night's torrential rain but each
of them is playing a losing game.

Hard Times in the Limestone Country

Not enough wood to coffin the body of a child
or build a gallows to hang a man from
not enough water to drown him in
not enough clay to cover his bones with earth
and nothing to wipe the shit from his arse
or cleanse the blood from what's left of his corpse
but motheaten tatters and sponges of stone

Happening

"Poetry makes nothing happen" — W.H. Auden

He had his secretary go out and buy
the books: the collected works in English
of every poet since Geoffrey Chaucer's time,
and got a man to shelve the wall behind

186

his desk. He liked their look and focused
lights on them so that visiting giants
from the corporate world could gawk at them.
Every now and then he'd swivel round
and stare at them when no one else was there.
During that time, when he was engaged
in surfing the net for porn or pretending
he was sober and awake, they hated
the way he'd turned his back on them
and carefully avoided discussing them
with his mistress or members of the board.
All they wanted was to be read and loved
but never once did he lay hands on them
or scan a page. His secretary heard
the crash and when she ran inside she found him
buried beneath a mountain of shelves
and books. He was dead. Revenge is sweet.

Forensics

There's no wind today. Look at those columns
of smoke rising like pillars to heaven.
I have my doubts. I need some hard facts.
Then for an instant a fingerprint
suddenly smudges the mirror of the lake.
But I know if I send for forensics
they're always going to be late.

The Sacred Illness

Not the look in the eyes of Wordsworth's
infant trailing its clouds of glory;
nor the joy in the eyes
of the angel of the annunciation
bringing the good news to Mary;
nor the love shining in the eyes
of the Christ forgiving his enemies
on the cross but all of these and more
in the eyes of my daughter emerging
from paradise after a grand mal seizure.

Hope

I knew people were communicating
with one another high above my head
so there I'd stand in my short trousers
in the cutting, legs blotched red with stings
after braving the nettles, one ear pressed
against the wooden telegraph pole,
listening to the steady hum of the world
going about its business and hoping
all the time I'd hear something I was
never going to hear: a word in my ear.

Clouds and Trees

What I saw when a wind rose up out of nowhere
was not Great Birnam Wood on its way
to Dunsinane nor a suddenly restless
forestry plantation but a becalmed
cloud shadow beginning to sail slowly
across the flanks of distant Benevanagh.

The Stour

In the hot windowless loft
under the Bangor slates
James and Paddy took turns with the flail
to thresh the sheaves of oats
I had helped to stook.
Even now in my eightieth year
I still see them through the increasing stour.

Picking Fruit

You are always saying this doesn't go
with that when you talk about clothes
and, mostly, I suppose you are right.
So I think I might know what you'd say
if you were with me today picking fruit

under a sky filmed with a nebulous veil
of cloud: that the blue of the sky is
an entirely different shade of blue
to the blue of the fruit but that the bloom
on the blue of the sky matches exactly
the bloom on the blue of the sloes.

Saving the Corncrake

It was not Moses come again to part
the waters a wind darkens with islands
of racing shadows but Alexander
the contractor cutting the first swathe
through the sea of grass in William's meadow.

Lichen Again

I knew it was time
to put on a sweater
when I saw gooseflesh
on the granite boulder
that wasn't wearing
a thermal vest
for this summit weather.

Regeneration

Some of Cormac's new fencing posts that were
cut from an ash near the shores of the lake
have sprouted limbs and a rich crop of leaves.

Frost said that good fences make good neighbours
but I say the best neighbours make fences
that can regenerate themselves as trees.

Bee Orchid

The first one I ever found was trembling
in a sea breeze on a limestone headland
at St. John's Point. I got down on my knees
with my book to make sure it was what I
thought it was and to feast my eyes. When I
came back next day it was gone.
I think it was cows. The lark I heard sing
above me that day would certainly know
but he clams up when he reaches the ground.
What's the point of being a bee orchid,
no matter how good your disguise,
if you haven't got four wings and a sting
to escape the fate of being munched up by cows?

The Memory of Water

In memoriam George Kinsella 1958-2004

No one was ever going to break *you* in.
Not for you the snaffle or the curb.
You plunged into life as you plunged
into the sea at The Guillamene
with a laugh or a roar and every time
you surfaced we knew you were coming up
for more than just a mouthful of air.
Until the day death took hold of you the way
you once took hold of life and would not let go.
You broke our hearts and all we could do
was be glad we had hearts that could break
even though we all knew what was broken
could only be mended by you.
So now, George Kinsella, I utter your name
in this mouthful of air
borne beyond rage and grief
to the sea all we living share.
You will never stop surfacing there.

Pyrola Rotundifolia

Webb: *abundant, common, very frequent,*
frequent, occasional, rare, very rare.
That's how he classifies Ireland's flora.
And when I discovered this small white flower
with round leaves in a wood here I keyed it
out in Webb and found it was *very rare.*
So rare that even when I told you
I hesitated before I said where.

Guilt

The ewes are kneeling to crop
the new grass. Is this their way
of reminding me the church bell
is pealing and that I should
be on my way to Mass?

Heat Wave

Listen to the sound of me
crunching through snow
crusted with frost
on this searing August day
as I walk by an old stone wall
in Friary on a bed
of dry withered moss.

Identity Crisis

The moment when my binoculars
that were hung on a strap from my neck
spilled out from my half-open anorak
and swung to and fro the way I first saw
your breasts spill out of your bra and swing
to and fro was the moment you chose
to call me a bastard instead of a bitch.

Corrie

They say it happened a long time ago
when the glaciers were on the move
like the circus from town to town
and littered the landscape with rocks
and scooped out holes in the ground
and even left this dent in the hat of the clown.

Animal Husbandry

John has a few acres of bog and rock.
Mostly rock. His two cows are always breaking
out to go roaming for sweeter grass.
When I told him that limpets graze on rocks
and that their grazing range was three feet
he said maybe he should be taking his cows
to the limpet instead of to the bull.

Rust

The further you walk
down the slipway you'll see
how the mooring rings
get thinner and thinner
until the one at the end
looks like that Polo mint
you once held up in your fingers
to show me how long you could suck it
before it melted in your mouth.
The sea has a sweet tooth.

A View from the Ruins

What I see today when I look
west from Colum Cille's glen
is a mirror smudged with cat's paws
as Pangur Bán abandons
what's left of the scriptorium
for the lab of IBM.

Musk Oxen

Are those matted
shaggy-with-lichen
herds of erratics
on the move
across the tundra
towards the glacier
looking for their mother?

Self Mutilation

A gull that stands preening
itself on a stone
in the lake's mirror
suddenly amputates its left leg
at the same time as a swan
breaks the glass and decapitates
itself in the shallows.

The Unfalling Snow

I saw the huge flock of gulls whitening
the dump rise up against the slate-blue sky.
You suddenly tugged at my hand, shouted:
"Look, Granda, look at the unfalling snow!"

The Priest

In memory of Eugene McDermott

He loved the island like he loved his God
and loved its people even more than that.
Titles were abhorrent: father was a name
for begetters and his Father in Heaven.
Even His Holiness stuck in his throat.
He worshipped God in Churches not his own
and said Luther should be made a saint.
Faith like an island candle lit his face.

I stand by his grave in sight of his church
and the sea looking at the roofless walls
of Iniskeeragh stark as headstones
against the grey sky. Graveyard of hopes there,
graveyard of bodies under the sod here,
but all his own people, the people of God.

The Politician

He practised in the bedroom when his wife
was out. The Mirrorimage guru said:
Smile with your eyes as well as with your mouth
in case they think you are baring your teeth.
Eyes are a bonus and shedding a few tears
is one sure way of increasing your vote.
So he looked into eyes to make them feel
there was nothing on earth he could not do

when all he was thinking of was how
he could manage to add another egg
to the eggs someone was sitting on for him
in a tax-free haven in the Caribbean
and picturing his mistress that night in bed
doing more than fondling his lacquered head.

The Patriot

They parse and analyse his paragraphs
to no avail. He speaks two languages,
both of them different but yet the same.
His favourite pet is the chameleon.
He has two faces: one is never seen
except by those who have two faces too
and when he shows his teeth no one is sure
whether it is a smile or displeasure.

Alter egos, as every mother knows,
resemble twins and never like to part
unless their heads can overrule their hearts.
So when the talks drag on, then break for tea,
it causes no surprise when he's descried
hurrying off to meet himself outside.

The Bishop

He needed sinners like he needed love
in case they thought it was a sinecure.
That was easy: he could rely on sin
but being humble when they knelt to kiss
his ring, even call him lord, that was hard
for someone like him whose peasant father
was staunchly republican and hated
every landlord like his son hated sin.

Administration: he was good at that
and now he claims to know their minds better
than he knows his own but still dreams of one
who thought of nothing but of love and sin.
A time before law-suits, profit and loss,
when wearing a cross was his only cross.

Once Upon a Time

there was a sin for which you went to Hell
double-quick they said. None of the others
seemed to matter quite so much: to tell
a lie, to swear, or hate the Smiths. Mother

told him all about the stork but not about
the pin-ups who showed more than just a leg
or why a girl who mysteriously filled out
like an inflated doll and whose name was Peg

did something mysterious to him too—
something he liked but others roared at him was lust.
He heard them, often, sitting in the pew
with Dad but had to take much of it on trust

until some boys told him a thing or two
that came in useful when he married Sue.

And a Very Long Time Ago

When women crossed their legs he closed his eyes
and prayed: sex is sin in so many ways:
in scented bodies and in glimpsed white thighs.
Often he cried for his childhood days.

Night after night he thought of death and hell,
dreamed of finding the perfect confessor;
he made long lists of sins he'd have to tell
and cursed Satan for being his oppressor.

But things went wrong and he began to drink.
The lusts of boyhood burned him fiercely now
in middle age; he called his mum a sow,

got married late, and crucified his wife.
Appetites rode him: he couldn't pray or think.
He was happy for the first time in his life.

Daisies

When she offered him her puckered lips
for a kiss he thought of the red tips
of closed daisies before they'd been prized
open by the hot tongue of the sun.

Synaesthesia

The snowy track is sullied with the prints
of Peter's feet and scattered wisps of hay.

He was foddering beasts here earlier today.
The wind has turned South since yesterday

and when I stop to listen to the crinkle
and crackle of ice beginning to melt

on Lough Eske I suddenly feel the heat
of a disintegrating red-hot coal fire.

Easaranca

The waterfall that turned
white with fear
and roared for help

as it plunged
over the edge of the cliff
regains its colour

but loses its voice
when it sees
the state of itself
in the pool at its feet.

Widower

He still sees an odd one maybe stuck
in a gap beside what's left of a house:
a rusted old cast-iron bedhead.

This one shakes with every gust from Trusk More.
Is it remembering nights when it shook
like his bed once shook under him and her?

Seurat

If you want to know
what influenced him most
you will have to hurry
and look at the pointillism
of the hawthorn hedge
stippled with infant buds
before it moves
into a completely new phase.

The Somme Survivor

They were fencing that day. Down by the sheugh
in Carn. Himself and his father and James.
They noticed he hardly opened his mouth
all day, put it down to the drink again.
Then the Yank passed by and took the photograph. Everyone,
including himself, is smiling

but he's standing stiffly to attention
with his hands by his sides as if he was
on the parade ground and somehow you sense
from the lie in his eyes to the eye
of the camera that he may not be
smiling but clenching his teeth. They finished
the fencing that day but neither of them
ever asked him to work with barbed wire again.

Mists

There's sea mist, hill mist, bog mist.
They're all shades of grey and taste
of the places they shroud.
But the mist that enveloped me
the day they manhandled her
to her knees in the byre
and opened a geyser
in her head was different.
It tasted of blood and was red.

R.S. Thomas

He would have liked them, I suppose.
They had nothing to say. Like God and the dead.
Living people were a different matter.
Until in that apocalyptic photograph
of him birdwatching on Anglesey in old age
he looked like one: God's scarecrow in Wales
frightening men and birds. And as sparse of words.

Song At The End Of Time

Let it never be said of me
as it was of others who sang
that they only sang of their love

when what they loved was dead.
So I set it down today
on paper in black and white
while I am still alive
though the scythesman is at the gate.
This is the woman I chose
against the voices of doubt
to lay her head on the pillow
beside mine in the marriage bed
and out of the clay of flesh
and the confessional dark
nurture a flower
even if sometimes I teetered
on the edge of an abyss
before love's tether tightened
again and drew me back
to the strong-minded woman who
mixed the earth I saw on graves
into her laughter and song,
shook affectation out of me
like a dog shakes its wet coat,
feared neither priest nor pope,
took country and religion
with more than a pinch of salt
and bore me the children
whose children I hope
will carry the seeds of our union
into the hearts of the children
of children yet to be born.
I open my mouth and shout it
so that everyone can hear.
Love, that will take on time,
even edge it towards fear,
love is here for the woman
whose virtues I sing.
The woman who is my wife.

Austerities

Soil is the flesh of rock but they knew
it would never flourish there.
So they chose this rock
in the sea and lived
like beetles in its crevices.
Gravity was the weight
of their sins but prayer
took them into the empyrean.
Sensuality was everywhere:
they heard the tongue of the sea
in the mouth of the cave,
saw in the swells the shapes
of thighs, buttocks, breasts
swathed in chiffon and lace.
An angry God berated them.
In his spittle they tasted
the salt of his tears.
And diet? Bread and water was
a feast when all they wanted was
what sustained the pure spirit.
Even skin and bone was
an impediment to soul.
They were proud of their pellets:
small and hard as their rosary beads.
Mountains, deserts, rock stacks:
outposts of heaven on earth.
Who will man them today?

The Walking Stick

Look, you said, and pointed down at the sand,
someone has been here with a walking stick

but I said if they were they must have been
shoeless and had three-toed feet and with that

a flock of oyster catchers stopped probing
the strand with their bills and took to the air.

Colour Co-Ordination

I never saw Thady with his cap off
except once at that funeral Mass.
The big bald head was a sickly white
in contrast to the deep brown of his face
and I knew it mightn't see the light of day
until he next crossed the mountain to Mass.
The last time I saw him was on the day
of his wake and I noticed how closely
death had matched the colour of his face
to the pillow and sheets and to his head.

Walking On Air Again In Old Age

Soft tussocks of grass and moss deflate
under our feet as the spring tide seethes

up the dry strand not far below us.
We listen to the hiss of escaping air

but it is only after we have clambered
over the locked gate in the wooden fence

that we suddenly rediscover
the difference between helping and holding hands.

The Artist

He painted landscapes so pure and pristine
they might have been still wet with morning mist.
But what's this? Are these two hillocks or a pair
of asymmetric breasts and what strange shape
is that emerging amorphously
from impasto like a sculpture from stone?
And why does that boulder appear to be
deliquescing into blood-red frog spawn?

The critics raved, the dealers wanted more,
but when he died the experts took a look
and found his canvases were palimpsests.
Everything he painted he painted twice:
once to try and drive the furies away
and once to keep his creditors at bay.

Schrödinger's Cat

Remembering them means nothing to the dead
whatever it may mean to those alive.
What point is there in dreaming of a poem
of yours being read a hundred years from now,
of scholars taking down your books from shelves
deeper in dust than what will then be you?
What's done or said will never comfort you.

Maybe the stories will outlive your words:
how sheepmen heard you reading poems to ewes,
watched you listening for voices from a cloud.
Some may have loved you. Not for what you wrote
but for the way your eyes would suddenly
become Chinese each time you laughed or tried
to force a smile in family photographs.

No matter where you are, if anywhere,
these are the things that you will never hear.
Not even love that pierces hearts of stone
will penetrate the clay that clogs your ears.
And so I practise for oblivion
by writing what's unread to get the feel
of what it's like being dead when I'm alive.

In Memory of Naoise 1993-2002

Sleep, my dearest, sleep and leave us
here to dream of a world we may not
enter with the world in our hearts.

Sleep, my dearest, sleep and in your dreams
know this: the only Heaven we knew
was the Heaven on earth of you.

Africa

She is crying on the box.
Her child is clutched to her breast.
You watch its black stick arms
fail again with the flies.
Tears trickle down the mother's cheeks.
And then she wets the tip
of her forefinger and moistens
the lips of the child
with the salt of her tears.
It never opens its eyes.

Jet

You said the sky was perfectly blue
with not even a wisp of a cloud and
it was except for a pulled thread
where it had snagged itself on Errigal.

North

Here come the bands.
Orange or green?
You can hear their colour
long before they're seen.

The Important Thing

Look how they've hosed all the blood from the street,
tidied away every sign that might force us
to face what was here is what we are,
so that the camera can focus on
the important thing: the entrails of a car.

The Golden Years

Knowing that you are old is not just being
grey and full of sleep in a dreamy Yeatsian way,

it's not just having to halt to draw breath
on every landing on the long way

up the hospital stairs or constantly
keep looking at mountains you'll never again climb,

it's not just hearing someone fail to suppress
a laugh when they ask you what age you are

and you answer proudly eighty-one and a half,
and it's not just watching your body disintegrate

and your mind beginning to acquire a mind of its own
and finding out that yes you're a man and have a prostate,

knowing that you are old is when they begin
to ask someone else how you are when you're there.

The Masochist

So here I am again, an old fool, writing
about sorrow, suffering, death, in a poem
that will hardly earn me the price of a trinket
or add joy to the lives of the few who'll read it.
Why then do I never want what I do to end?

Index of First Lines

come in at the ends of their tethers, 130
Consider the unblinking perfection, 119

Did they once cry for their mothers, 22

Even in this guttering light, 184
Even then I thought of him as Joseph, 65
Even though it lay fallow for years now, 71
Even though you're still afraid of horses, 99

Far out over the sea, 146
Farmers say you can't eat the scenery, 155
Fermanagh: half in and half out, 59
For ages, buried in dusty bric-à-brac, 52
For centuries I have been quaking, 128
For fifty years he travelled light into, 9
For years, deciding that he knew it all, 44

God, you said, with a sweep of your hand, 143
Going to sleep at night sometimes he, 46
Grass still bent under the weight, 131

H.M.H. The mustered consonants stand, 60
Hand in hand, 147
has always known how to make an art out, 175
has spent a lifetime trying to perfect, 88
has the unhurried gait of, 51
He brought it back after his first visit, 175
He came today to take away her things, 49
He could forget the malice of cities, 15
He could not tell you why, 7
He did it in the dark: that handsome face, 124
He had his secretary go out and buy, 186
He is ploughing, 13
He left her clearing out an old wardrobe, 179

He lived alone till she arrived and she, 45
He lives alone in the shadow of, 15
He looked leonine with that mane of hair, 171
He loved the island like he loved his God, 198
He needed sinners like he needed love, 200
He painted landscapes so pure and pristine, 209
He practised in the bedroom when his wife, 198
He rode into the scrub lands of that last, 20
He still sees an odd one maybe stuck, 203
He treads water to get, 41
He used to lift me high above his head, 60
He was never one for showing emotion, 180
He would have liked them, I suppose, 205
He's walking on a woodland track, 183
Here come the bands, 212
Here I am again space-walking, 142
Here I am back in my own place again, 163
His best friend told him that he'd picked his nose, 120
History walled them out. For three centuries, 22
How beautiful the archway framing, 180
How do I know that the wrecked blue boat, 56

I am eye-level with harebells, 55
I bought my first one from a man I knew, 63
I came out of you, protesting, a long, 104
I could talk for hours about mountains, lakes, 183
I found your mother there and pine martens, 97
I hardly knew him: I was only six, 47
I hear the sound of felling in the glen, 103
I helped to vest him in the sacristy, 116
I knew it was time, 190
I knew people were communicating, 188
I knew the storm that thrashed, 185
I knew when I'd said it that I'd rubbed you the wrong way, 169
I know him. And I know his fields, 122

Myself and the dog. A thorn, 44

So here I am again, an old fool, writing, 213
So much of his life was spent in this room, 48
Soft tussocks of grass and moss deflate, 209
Soil is the flesh of rock but they knew, 207
Some of Cormac's new fencing posts that were, 191
Somehow the tumbling paddy always took, 95
Something that doesn't belong up here any, 30
Starved of colour after the long winter, 183
Steam from the Mucker dung-heap mists his mind, 24
Such amorous passion in the long grass,, 154
Such jealousies as once their partings bred, 181
Summers we went west to Donegal and, 69
Sun, rain, snow, storm; the derision of crows, 114
Sweeney was full of it and long before, 125

That August day when I found, 149
That big drunken man over there, 93
that he may always find wonder, 133
that he may one day find enlightenment, 138
That time I followed the arrows a bird, 141
That time will come. We won't have long to wait, 166
The big bull calf, all sea legs after nine, 119
The blades of the oars, 153
The brent geese appear and disappear, 147
The day that I went up to Meenaguise, 136
The day you told me I had two faces, 142
The days of cattle-raiding dawn campaigns, 70
The dog noses a steaming bag lumped, 84
The ewes are kneeling to crop, 193
The eyes of the girl with the pigtail, 144
The first crocuses are, 38
The first one I ever found was trembling, 191
The five-fingered palmate, 168
The further you walk, 196
The glen was full of barking dogs but you, 82

Whatever it is, it's hardly the weather, 111
When I saw them in the distance I said, 149
When I took ages today, 148
When it's not drawing circles and half circles, 144
When she offered him her puckered lips, 202
When someone remarks you look like me why do, 156
When women crossed their legs he closed his eyes, 201
Who laid that timber plank across the burn, 79
Who's that dour man with the quarried face and, 94

Yes. I remember that day. Blue Stack was, 101
Yesterday, for some reason I couldn't, 38
You are always saying this doesn't go, 189
You came up in the doctor's trawl that day:, 26
You cut them dripping, 75
You have grown out of our reach, 29
You learned to pick your steps from stone to stone:, 62
You never played the other side but still, 68
You said the sky was perfectly blue, 212
You went there first with us one April day, 97
You were not black because your skin was black, 67
Your cold white hands that, 182
Your small hand, warm and vulnerable and, 100

224

Printed in the United Kingdom
by Lightning Source UK Ltd.
120767UK00001B/269